Sanity Savers:

Help for Frazzled Parents

Cheryl Zarra

"Sanity Savers: Help for Frazzled Parents," ISBN 1-58939-218-3.

Library of Congress Control Number: 2002107754.

Published 2002 by Virtualbookworm.com Publishing Inc., P.O. Box 9949, College Station, TX , 77842, US. ©2002 S. L. Cullars. All rights reserved. No part of this publication may be reproduced, stored in a retrieval system, or transmitted in any form or by any means, electronic, mechanical, recording or otherwise, without the prior written permission of S. L. Cullars.

Manufactured in the United States of America.

No liability will be assumed for damages resulting from the use of the information contained herein. Always consult a physician before making changes to your child's diet or routine.

Table of Contents

Acknowledgments

Writing this book while playing with and helping my toddler son figure out the world in which he lives in, caring for my infant daughter in addition to a neighbor's infant daughter was not an easy task. I would like to take a moment to thank a few people who have helped me make the dream of sharing the love and joy of parenting through this book possible.

First and foremost I would like to thank my loving and supportive husband, Dave, who on many occasions took care of the kids and gave me time to write. If it were not for him this book would still be in the "I really should write some of this stuff down" stage. Not only did he support my efforts to actually write this book he often lovingly commented on the many activities I did with my son during his first few years of his life as well as my daughter. He always made me feel that the things I did with our children both small and grand would positively influence them forever.

To my children, Nicholas and Angela, I thank you for giving me the opportunity to be a Mommy in every sense of the word. For happily listening to my off-key voice while I sang to you. For not looking embarrassed when I would dance or sing in public. And for letting me try out many activities with you some in the experimental stages with interesting outcomes.

Finally, to those parents who gave their tips to share with others – thank you!

Introduction

Going from two incomes to one is tough. Most couples are both working in order to take care of the family's basic needs. If you really want to stay home to raise your children you will have to look into your family budget and heart's desire and be willing to make some big changes and great sacrifices. In making your decision just remember that the sacrifices you make today will be paid back ten-fold when you see the way your child has grown into a loving and responsible person. And smile at the fact that you have played the biggest part in one of life's greatest accomplishments.

Staying home to raise your children is the most rewarding yet frustrating career you will ever embark on. Each day brings about the opportunity for you to help little ones find their way around the world, make sense of it all and have fun in the process. While this sounds exciting I will not sugar coat the reality of this career choice – some days are so wonderful that you wish you could freeze them and repeat them day in and day out forever and other days will have you hoping that their 18th birthday would come tomorrow so they can unwrap their brand new suitcase packed and ready to go! Don't despair; I have put together for you much of the information you will need to know to have a more fulfilling time in the career of your choice. As a former Early Childhood Educator and mother of two I have plenty of experience with day-to-day life with these little wonders. I have made both excellent choices as well as those that should have never left the early stages of the thought process in my mind. Let me share with you those that worked for me and those that failed miserably. I hope this information can help you to make good days great and bad days better.

I would now like to share with you a little story that has crossed my path many times in many variations. I like to refer to this story whenever I want to justify my daily accomplishments as a stay at home parent. The author is unknown and I have taken a few editorial liberties to suit my experiences.

On Being a Mom

My husband came home today and saw me sitting on the couch, toddler on one knee and baby nursing on the opposite breast. I was trying to turn the pages of a book with the hand not attached to the infant while listening to the sound of the stove buzzer, which would indicate that tonight's dinner was at the stage between "well done" and "the dogs get tonight's entrée". My husband looked at me innocently and asked "So, did you do anything today?"

It's a good thing that most of my appendages were otherwise occupied, as I was unable to jump up and throttle him to death. This was probably for the best, as I assume that asking a stupid question is not grounds for murder in this country.

Let me back things up just a bit and explain what led me to this point in my life. I was not always bordering on the brink of insanity. On the contrary, a mere four years ago, I had a good job, steady income, and a vehicle that could not seat a professional sports team and me comfortably. I watched television shows that were not hosted by singing puppets. I went to bed later than nine at night, not much but a little later anyway. I also preferred sex to sleeping in.

What happened to me? Well, I saw two lines in the tester window instead of one! I have since traded my satin and lace lingerie for cotton briefs and a nursing bra. My idea of privacy is getting to use the bathroom without a three year old banging on the door and the baby playing with a piece of toilet paper on my lap. Goodbye movies rated "R" and hello to Dragon Tales and Little Bear. And I now understand that the term "Stay at home Mom" does not refer to a parent who no longer works outside the house, rather one who never seems to get out the front door.

So here I sit, children in hand wondering, how to answer my beloved husband. DID I DO ANYTHING TODAY? Well, I think I did, although not much seems to have gotten accomplished. I shared breakfast with a handsome young man. Of course breakfast consisted of dry cereal and left over cookie crumbs found in the bottom of the cookie tin. The handsome young man is all of 35 inches tall and only gets excited at the sight of construction equipment and ice cream. I got to take a relaxing stroll outdoors. Of course I had to look for frogs and bugs, and had to stop to smell each dandelion along the way. I successfully washed one load of laundry, moved the load that was in the washer into the dryer and the dryer load into the basket. The load that was in the basket is now spread out on the bed, awaiting my bedtime decision to actually put the clothes away or merely move them to the top of the dresser. I did read two or three books. Of course Dickens and Shakespeare cannot take credit for these works, as I have moved to the works of Seuss and Numeroff. I don't think I will be making any trips to the adult section of the library anytime soon. In between I dusted, wiped, organized and rearranged. I kissed away the ouches and washed away the tears. I stopped the onset of diaper rash, scolded, praised, hugged and had my patience tested all before noon.

Did I do anything today? You Bet! I will now understand what people mean when they say that parenting is the hardest job they will ever have. In my life before diapers I was able to meet the shortest of deadlines and the heaviest of workloads. I was able to educate adults how to use software on many different platforms. Yet I am unable to teach a 3 yr old how to use the potty. I was also once able to navigate streets while looking for a decent radio station, but now I can't get the wheels on my stroller to all go in the same direction.

So, in response to my husband's inquiry, yes I did do something today. In fact, I am one step closer to one of life's greatest accomplishments. No, I didn't find a cure for cancer, but I did hold a miracle in my arms, two in fact. My children are my greatest accomplishment and the opportunity to raise them is my greatest challenge. I don't know if my children will grow up to be great leaders or world-class brain surgeons. Frankly, I don't care as long as they grow up to be good people.

Children really do make life interesting.

Chapter 1
Parenting Basics

I f you were to look up the word "child" in the dictionary you would undoubtedly find that it refers to a person between infancy and adolescence who is strongly influenced by other people, places and experiences. Parents have a HUGE responsibility to see to it that their children, who are influenced by everything they come in contact with, learn and grow in a safe, caring and nurturing environment. Now I pose the big question - How will you do this while trying to maintain a household and not go crazy in the process? No clue? Well, lucky for you I am here to help. First of all you need to master the "basics" so that everyday life with little ones is a pleasure and not a chore.

In this first chapter I touch upon a few "basics" that are in my opinion the most important ones you will need to understand in order to carry on in a safe and productive manor. So sit back, take a deep breath and start reading. You'll get through this ok. Really!

Child Proofing Your Home

While there are many child proofing books you could purchase or companies you can hire that will come to your home and "child proof" for you, there are simple and less expensive common sense things you can do to make your home and yard a safe place for your children to play and grow.

I affectionately refer to the physical environment both indoors and out where you and your children will spend your time together as "The Learning Grounds". The sooner you have your learning grounds child proofed the happier and safer both you and your children will be.

Indoor Learning Grounds

This place, be it one room, a few rooms or your whole house is a potential hazard to your children. I cannot stress this enough – CHILD PROOF this area. Whether you have crawlers or walkers get down on your hands and knees so you can see this area as they do. Put yourself in their shoes and think of everything you see as a toy – now is it safe? If not then move it, cover it or put it away. Children are very crafty. Just because you put something slightly out of their reach does not mean it is unreachable. This may mean some big changes to your décor but it is better to be safe than sorry. You do not want to spend your days telling your children "No, don't touch that!" or getting angry and upset because your sweet angels have broken every Hummel you have on display. You also don't want to make avoidable trips to the emergency room because an outlet was not properly covered or the sharp corner of the coffee table was not softened or moved. Your house can go back to being your showplace when the kids have grown until then rearrange and make it safe. It may take some creativity on your part but you can still have a little style and be child safe.

When dealing with sleeping/resting areas make sure cribs, cots, beds, or mats have also been inspected for potential hazards. Check to make sure they meet all safety standards. Don't put cribs, pack-n-plays, cots or any other sleeping furniture near dressers, shelves or tempting knick-knacks. Please, please be wary of cords on window blinds, an often-overlooked household hazard. Safety First makes nice cord wind-ups and furniture strips for attaching dressers and shelves to the walls, purchase a few and save a life.

If you have multi levels to your home be sure to have gates for the steps and refrain from putting anything near your windows that your children can climb on to get to them. Keep all windows locked and install window gates for added safety.

Outdoor Learning Grounds

Make sure this area is just as safe as the learning grounds inside of your home. Hopefully you will have a fenced in area for the children to play in. If you do be sure the fence is intact and it has a lock on the gate high enough that the children will have difficulty reaching it without your observation. Keep all outdoor toys as clean as possible (a plastic box with holes in the bottom for drainage is a good place to store them) and remove broken ones as they deteriorate. If you have a sandbox make sure it has a cover so the neighborhood cats don't use it as their personal bathroom. Keep the grass trimmed and remove any animal droppings as soon as they are created from the play area if you have dogs that are free to roam in the same play space as the children.

With regard to our four legged furry friends please be sure to keep all of your pets up to date on all of their vaccines and the minute you sense trouble or aggression from any animal quickly remove said animal from the children and keep him/her locked in a safe area. Pets are nice companions and often love to play with children, they are also a great way to teach children about love, friendship and responsibility but each animal has a different temperament and even the most affectionate of pets can only stand so much "love" and teasing from small children – always keep an eye out for this.

If you are still not sure if your house and yard is ready to handle those tiny inquisitive hands, look in your local phone book for specialized companies that come out and evaluate your home for safety. If you do not have such a listing in your local directory go on-line and look up "child proofing". You are bound to find that many of these companies advertise on the Internet. If they are not local enough to pay you a visit you can purchase comprehensive checklists and kits to further safety proof your home.

The Routine

If you do nothing else, besides child proofing your home of course, create a few routines and stick to them. Routines play a big part in a relaxed environment especially with children 3 and under. Young children thrive on routines, they need a sense of security in knowing what to expect. I do not mean that at 12:02 every day everyone will eat the same lunch at the same time. Do not lock yourself or the children into set times. Instead have predictable <u>patterns </u>in your daily events. Children, although not always happy about it, will get accustomed to rest time following lunch and a story if repeated in the same order enough times. Another example, If you sing "Row, Row, Row Your Boat" while you clean up to get ready for lunch each day you will soon find that if you simply sing this song your little ones will automatically begin to clean up in anticipation of lunch. Just by setting up this routine you will find that getting your kids to clean up and get ready for lunch will no longer be a struggle.

How Children's Play Develops from Birth to Age 5

There is nothing more frustrating to a child or you than trying to get him to accomplish something he is not yet capable of doing. You need to understand your child's abilities and limitations to avoid such frustrations. I have outlined the basic characteristics of children's play development from birth to age five for you. This information has been derived from my formal education, my many years of teaching and of course, being a Mom.

Whatever the age or stage of your child enjoy them as they pass from one stage to the next. If you would like to know more detail about each stage of child development you need to look no further than your local library or bookstore. There are countless books out there that go into great detail about child-development. Another avenue to investigate regarding child development is your local college. They will usually offer mini-courses on this topic just for parents. Always keep in mind that each child develops at his/her own pace so don't rush them!

Birth to 12 Months

From birth until about one year of age babies develop at an incredible rate. Each day these little wonders gain more and more control over their bodies. They learn how to hold up their heads; roll over; sit unassisted; crawl; and for some they can walk. During this time babies learn about their bodies. They are aware of their fingers and toes and find much amusement in playing with them. They even begin to recognize their name. Communication skills are also developing. At first babies cry to have their needs met. Later they babble, razz their tongues and say mama and dada. As time passes they play with more and more sounds and begin to connect them to a few close people and objects.

12 Months to 3 Years

Call them Waddlers or Toddlers but children this age are on the move! For the next two years these little darlings are constantly working on their coordination and language skills. They thrive on routines, as a sense of security so be sure to include them in your day-to-day doings. They are becoming more independent and often demand to do things for themselves. Give them plenty of opportunities

Sanity Savers For Frazzled Parents

to make their own decisions such as "Would you like to have milk in your red cup or blue cup?"

They are also very curious and are constantly exploring their environment and the objects within. They are intent on figuring out how a toy works, what happens to it when they drop it, throw it or bang it. Note: Make sure toys are sturdy enough to handle these investigations.

They touch, taste, listen and look at everything! Expect it and plan for it by providing a safe hands-on environment with as many harmless things to explore. I hope I don't have to tell you to supervise this curious age at all times, no matter how safe you think you have made it, accidents can and will happen.

The young Waddler/Toddler group, 12 to about 24 months, tend to play alongside others rather than with them in a collaborative way. And by all means, do not expect them to share; it is not in their make-up at this time. If you have a group of children this age or a mix together be sure to provide ample play toys to avoid as many "Mine" moments as possible.

A final note on this age group, don't be surprised if your child latches on to a particular object say a blanket or stuffed toy and totes it around everywhere. It is inevitable and harmless. It simply provides them with a sense of security.

3 Years to 5 Years

Imagination! Imagination! Imagination! Need I say more? Ok I will. Their imaginations are beginning to take over their play at the same time as cooperative play and the development of friendships. Children this age tend to imitate familiar roles and they embellish on them in the most interesting ways. Before you know it Barber/Beauty shops have taken over your dining room while a grocery store or restaurant invades your kitchen. Don't be alarmed if a construction site enters your living room just be prepared to put on a hard hat and get to work. They like to make up their own games and use the same object to represent a number of real life items.

Their large and small motor skills are becoming fine tuned as they play with smaller toys. Their language skills develop even further as they attach words to actions and ideas.

Imaginary friends may begin to appear at your dinner table. Just be sure to set an extra plate but don't fall for the old "My friend needs a dessert too." As you know your child will have to help him eat it. If you do fall for the old dessert trick make sure your child's imaginary friend has eaten all of his or her dinner first. This is such a fun time!

Chapter 2
Tips, Tricks and Advice from Parents

Parenting Tips

Did you ever wonder how other parents get their children to eat vegetables, clean up their toys, and remain in bed after tucking them in? I have presented many Moms and Dads with these and other questions. It is here that I share with you the tips and tricks I have learned over my many years of teaching young children whether it was hands on trial and error or direct communications with the many parents of the children in my care, my years of experience of being a Mom as well as the answers from the Moms and Dads who were gracious enough to share their wisdom for the making of this book.

Baby Bows

"I have a two month old baby girl. I like to dress her up but when I put a little bow or clip on her hair it slides right off. I found out that to make it stay on without

sliding off. Just put a little piece of regular sponge with the hair in the middle of the clip then snap the clip on in place. Now she can dress up & look like a pretty little girl."

Hope M., Mommy of One, Texas

Beach Runaways

The warm sun and a tired parent do not mix. If your child has fallen asleep on the blanket next to you and you fear nodding off and missing them if they wake here is a tip to keep you on your toes.

Tie a string on your wrist and your child's ankle. If he wakes and moves you will know about it.

Patricia I., Mommy of Three, NJ

Big Kid Beds – Making the move

How to make this sometimes scary transition not so scary.

"When I transferred my 2 year old daughter to a 'big girl bed' I use to sing this song so she wouldn't cry. "You're a big girl now and its time to go to sleep. You're a big girl now and your not gonna cry, cuz your a BIG girl now." It was a simple song I sang every night for about a year, but it worked every time."

Toni, Mommy of One

Biting

Children bite for many reasons. Usually it is the young children around the age of 15 months to 2 ½ years of age. They may bite to get someone's attention, because they want a particular toy another is playing with, or they get so angry that they just bite to vent. Although a few moms wrote in that they bit their children back on the hand to show them how it feels I don't like it. Children this young do not understand that logic. Use it if you feel ok with it but I prefer these tips.

Tell your child "No" in a stern voice tell them that they are to bite food only. Express for them in words what it is they are trying to say. They just don't have the vocabulary to put their feelings into words.

Express disappointment in their behavior only and not them personally. Remove your child from the situation and tell them that it is wrong to bite. Tell them that they have to use words not teeth to get what they want. Give them a brief time out to help them cool down and then have them apologize to the child they bit.

Cleaning up the Toys

If you are a neat freak nothing will irk you more than to see toys constantly scattered throughout your home or in your child's special play area. Here are a few pointers to get those little hands helping.

Move to the music. Sing a clean up song. It doesn't have to make much sense or rhyme just sing and clean. "La, La, La Clean up" usually worked for my son. We would sing it over and over again until we both picked up all the toys. I used the song in conjunction with the next tip.

Toy Jail. If your child won't pick them up put them in jail. Use a table or a clear storage container with a lid. If your child refuses to pick up the toys simply put it in toy jail. Indicate that the toy is to remain there for two days. Leave the toy jail in plane view so your child can still see the toy. Remember if you take it away and put it out of sight it becomes forgotten and your point does not get across. After the two days are up release the toy under the condition that it is to be put away when finished with. I love this one. It really worked for my son.

Break out with the reward chart. Reward charts work well for many situations. When your child has helped to clean up let them put a sticker on their chart. After four successive stickers or marks give them a small treat i.e. a book, an extra 15 minutes of playtime before bed, a special sticker, lunch out at their favorite place (hopefully this is a picnic in the yard)... You get the idea.

For easy toy clean up, keep a medium size box in each room that toys are allowed in for fast and easy toy clean up.

Diaper Rash

Whether it is teething or simply sensitive skin, a diaper rash is no fun for parent or child. Here are a few hints to keep her bottom comfy.

Let them go naked. After cleaning the skin with warm water, gently dry the area with a cloth and let the fresh air dry them out. A bit of cornstarch can help as well. Being closed up in a diaper makes for moist conditions not pleasant for a diaper rash.

Ease up on the commercial wipes. Even the ones for sensitive skin can be harsh. Just use warm water and either a clean cloth or tissues.

"I am a mother of a one year old and quite regularly she get's a very bad diaper rash. After, taking her back and forth to the doctor and still no luck, I had just about given up. One day I was talking to a older woman at the pharmacy when the topic came up and she told me to rub

a little bit of Maalox on my daughter's bottom. Needless, to say it worked and still works like a charm!"

       Layla R., Mommy of One, Georgia

Dislikes Car Seat

If your little one cries each time you put him in a car seat for a quick trip to the store or a long ride to visit family and friends try these tips to make the ride more pleasurable.

Get a mirror. If your child sits rear facing try using a mirror so that your baby can see both himself and you.

Familiarize your child with the car seat by bringing it into the house and let him explore it. Use it for nap time, feed him in it or even play a game using it.

Hang something interesting in the view of your child. The back of a plain seat is not all that interesting to look at. If your child faces forward place something of interest to view over the seat in front.

Toys. Provide your child with toys attached to the seat with short strings so that if they fall to the side they can get to them.

Door Slammers

Children love to slam doors. Here is a great tip to soften the blow.

Put a hand towel over the top of the door. That way when they go to slam the door it doesn't close all the way.

Ease the Boo-Boos

When your child gets a bump getting them to keep ice on the boo-boo is not often easy. Here are two helpful tips.

"Freeze plastic shaped ice-cubes such as flowers or fish. These are usually found in the seasonal section of any department store in the spring and summer. Kids like to hold these colorful netted bags of coolness on their bumps. They also don't make the watery mess of regular ice-cubes."

Barbara Slein, Mommy of Three, New Jersey

Use colorful ice-cubes in a baggie. Make colored ice in trays by adding food color. When needed place a few cubes in a baggie and then in another baggie. Kids love color and the double baggie will allow them to hold the ice without getting soggy.

Fear of Monsters

Children have a very vivid imagination and before you know it familiar sounds take on personalities all their own. Soon a family of monsters will invade the night and often take up refuge in your child's room. The most popular places are under the bed and in the closet. Here are a few ways to help rid your child's room of monsters.

Take an empty spray bottle and fill it with water. You can add a breath mint for smell if you like. Tell you child that it is special monster spray and wherever you spray it the monsters will disappear.

Decorate a small flashlight with stickers. Tell your child that this special flashlight has magic powers and once you flash the light on a particular part of the room the monsters leave.

Make up a silly word like Jubba-Jubba. Explain to your child that if you say these magic words three times all the monsters go home. If you child ever thinks that there is a monster still lurking about they can just repeat these words and poof! The monsters vanish.

"When my kids were afraid of monsters under the bed, we made a monster repellent, made up of shiny confetti, (found at any craft store) and my children would blow it around their rooms. Makes a bit of a mess but a vacuum works wonders well worth a night's sleep."

Cindy O., Mommy of Three, MA

Fear of Thunder

The sky darkens and the rain begins to fall. Shortly after the rain you hear a loud clap of thunder and immediately little running feat and screeches of panic can be hear throughout the house. How can you calm a child down when you have no control over the weather? Try these solutions.

My son was afraid of the thunder until I old him that thunder is nothing more than clouds that are heavy with rain bumping into each other. The thunder is the sound of the clouds telling each other – "Excuse Me". And as they bumped each other rain fell to the ground. Will I win any science award? No, but it worked like a charm.

Explain the scientific reasoning for the sound of thunder. Personally I think this might confuse them. In my opinion keep it simple and silly. Remember if they laugh they can't cry.

Tell your child to count out loud between the claps of thunder. The higher the number the farther away the thunder is which means the storm is moving out and will soon be over.

Fear of Tweezers
Some children are so afraid of the tweezers that they will often times not show you a splinter in their hand. Here are two hints to ease the fear of tweezers.

Try putting a piece of scotch tape over the splinter and then peel off. This works for most surface splinters.

With your back to your child, take your child's arm or leg, wherever the splinter is and tuck it under your arm. This way they can't see what you are doing. Then sing some songs together until the splinter is out.

Grumpy Children
Is there a case of the grumps or crabby cakes in your house? Try these tips to lighten things up.

Put them in water. For babies as well as older children. Turn on the sprinkler, fill the pool, give them a bath or fill a dishpan for splashing outside. Water has a calming effect on kids as well as adults.

Make silly faces at each other.

Turn on the music and start dancing as wildly as you can. Sing silly verses to well loved songs. This is sure to bring a smile to your child's face.

Hitting

Hitting is another bad habit a child can easily fall into if they lack the vocabulary to express themselves. Here are a few tips to help with hitting.

Remove your child from the situation. Talk to your child and ask why they hit. Provide them with other solutions to getting what they are after.

Clapping. Tell your child that if he feels like he needs to hit something then have him clap his hands together to release his tension.

The pillow. Instead of hitting a person have your child hit a pillow.

Holding Breath

A mother of a 2 year old, wishing to be anonymous, wrote to me with these tips on how she got her son to stop holding his breath when he got upset. My son would hold his breath when he cried about the age of 2 as well. I tried tip number one but it only annoyed him so I stopped doing anything and he eventually grew out of it. If you toddler tries this with you, use one of these tips.

Blow a little air in his face. The shock will snap him out of it and he will breath again.

Let them go. Let them hold their breath the worst that will happen is that they will pass out and when that happens they will automatically breathe again.

Water. Sprinkle a bit of water in their face to jolt them back to reality.

Take them to see their pediatrician. They may have some other tips or medical advice for you.

Keeping baby/Child clothes Clean

If you hate stains on your kids' clothes try these tips.

"Hey, I learned it the hard way...if you don't like stained children's clothing, then at mealtimes, use bibs, and let them have only old clothing for play-clothes."

"For those stubborn stains on baby clothes, soak with Simple Green, from the automotive department of Wal-Mart Stores for 10 minutes, then wash."

Sharla R., Mommy of Five, Kansas

Misbehaving or simply Out of Control

Just when you think you are at your wits end with your child/children because they are not listening to you, they are running around and simply getting into trouble what do you do? Try these hints.

You may just need a break from each other. If you can't get a sitter or relative to come and relieve you for an hour or so then put them in their rooms for "Quiet Time" and breathe deep.

Be consistent with your rules. Don't give in because you are in a good mood. If the answer is no for a particular desire once the answer should be no each time. Inconsistency will cause your child to test your patience and will power.

Send them to their room for a time out to think about what they are doing. Talk to them about their behavior and tell them that it is unacceptable.

Check for food allergies. Some children act out if given too much sugar or certain food dyes. Always consult with your child's doctor before cutting anything from their diet.

"Break out the Reward Chart. Give them a sticker for every positive thing or pre-determined chore they do. At the end of the day count the stickers together. Daily or weekly provide them with a treat – something small."

Gina C., Mommy of Two, NJ

On the way out

Whether you are going to the doctor's office or on a visit to a friend or relative here is a must for all parents.

Pack an activity bag with crayons, paper, small toys, stickers etc and keep it in the car so busy hands can keep out of trouble wherever you go.

Pacifiers

Seeing a three-year-old walk around with a pacifier in his mouth is not pleasing to the eye nor is it necessary. I have even read in dental magazines that it is not good for the gums and teeth. So how do you nix the pacifier fix? Well, my son was never a pacifier baby. He simply did not want one. I tried to give them to him as a baby but he only played with them. I guess I should be thankful for not having to break that habit. My daughter on the other hand likes the pacifier to sleep with. Since she is only nine months old I am not looking to get rid of it yet but I am sure when the day arrives I will be looking towards these tips to help out.

Set limits. Slowly decrease the use of the pacifier during waking hours. If at all possible limit the use to sleep times. Keep your child as occupied as possible. When they get bored they will look for it.

Get creative. If you just take it away and tell him it is lost or someone stole it, they will simply latch onto something else and never let it out of their sight for fear of having it "ripped" from them. Instead try having the Pacifier Fairy pay your little one a visit. Tell your child that at night a special Pacifier Fairy will pay him a visit and take his pacifier to a Pacifier Play-Land and in return he will find a special surprise when he wakes. Then at night after your child falls asleep take the pacifier way and leave a special trinket in its place with a note from the Fairy thanking him for his pacifier.

Simply take it away. Let your child say goodbye to it and toss it. Of course with this way you may have to deal with a few extra tears at bedtime. If this does happen give your child something to cuddle. I am not sure I like this one but each child is different so why not.

Have a going away party for the pacifier. Go out and buy a helium balloon. Tie the pacifier to the end of the string. Have your child say goodbye to the pacifier and give it a kiss. Then let your child let go of the string to send it off. Once it is out of sight celebrate with a special treat.

Potty Training

Here is another one of those questions that every mom with a two plus year old asks – How can I help my child to potty train? Child development books, pediatricians and the like will all tell you the same thing. When they are ready they will do it. But to every mom out there they know there must be something they can do to speed up the process. Here is the feedback I received from the moms.

Let them go Naked. This is for the truly brave and bare floor. I was told that when they are naked they are more inclined to sit on the potty because they do not have to deal with the diaper/training pant and clothes. It is also supposed to give them a better sense of the "feeling" when they need to go or the "feeling" they get when they actually mess. Not for me but I've heard it works.

The little reinforcement. For some it is a sticker for others it may be a penny or a small treat. My son went for M&M's. He would get a plain one for sitting and trying and a peanut one for actually going.

The bigger picture. Use a chart and add a sticker each time they go on the potty and after a certain number of stickers they would be able to get a larger desired item for example a toy or lunch at Chuckee Cheese.

When #1 works and #2 is the problem because they refuse to sit long enough to let it happen, try reading them a story while on the potty. My son would sit on the potty and we would draw pictures on his Magnadoodle for the longest time. This helped because he was one for sitting about 30 seconds before jumping off saying he was finished.

Potty together. Let your child's stuffed friend sit on the other potty. My son would put his purple elephant on the little potty while he sat on the big potty. What really got him started though was to see his little sister sitting on the potty. One day I put his 7½-month-old sister on the potty for company and she actually went. This was enough to get my son to keep trying. I guess he figured if a baby could do it so could he. I didn't have the heart to tell him that it was shear coincidence that she went.

Steer clear of the desire to switch between the diaper and training pant. Choose one way and stick with it. You will only confuse them. I wanted to use up all my sons diapers while we used the training pants. I figured if I put the diapers on at night and the training pants on during the day it would be ok. One day he asked "Mom, what am I wearing a diaper or potty pants?" Right then I stopped using the diapers because I was afraid that if he thought he was wearing a diaper he would think it was ok to mess in them.

Books and videos. Some moms preferred books and videos on the subject. My son liked to watch them and hear the stories but they didn't do anything to make him "want" to go. Give them a try-they can't hurt.

Take it along. Once your child gets the hang of the potty try this for long or even short car trips. Put the potty seat in the car. If your child has to go, simply pull over and pull out the potty. First, line the potty bowl with a plastic bag to catch the "mess" this makes for easy discarding. If your child is old enough to "hold it" then you need not take along the potty seat but for those just starting out it does wonders for their self-confidence. There is nothing worse then telling your child there is no place to potty leaving them to have an accident in the car. They get upset, you get upset and in some instances you have just set potty training back a few weeks. They can become fearful of having accidents if they leave the house.

Hit the target. Try putting cheerios in the potty and let him try to move them around while peeing. They have a blast at this and it really does help with their aim.

Sink it! If you do not want to use cheerios to practice aiming try putting one square of toilet paper floating on the water, their goal is to sink it!

Keep extra pairs of underwear in the bathroom. If an accident does happen they will be able to change themselves without the embarrassment of having to ask you to get them clean underwear while giving them a sense of independence.

"I do have a creative child-rearing tip when it comes to potty training which is what we're going thru now. In stores they have those flushable "targets" for boys but I could stand buying something to just flush it so we would throw a Cheerio in the bowl and tell him to try and hit it. Sounds funny I know but it helped him to learn to keep it in the bowl. We also when they were first starting to use the potty give them one M&M for going pee and 2 for having a BM. My oldest got upset because he wasn't earning treats anymore so he got one for reminding the younger one to go."

Rachel, Mommy of 3, UK

Quieting A Crying Baby

First make sure all of their basic needs have been met. Ask yourself the following questions. Are they hungry, are they too hot or cold, do they need a diaper change, have they been burped, do they just need a little cuddling time. If all needs have been met or attempted try the following.

Run a vacuum cleaner or hair dryer. For some reason the noise from these two machines quiets them down. I do not know why but it worked for both of my kids.

Carry them in a football hold. Place your baby belly down across your arm with their head resting in the palm of your hand. The pressure on their belly may be enough to get out more gas. Even if they burped after their bottle some babies are more sensitive to extra gas than others and any little bit is discomforting. This gentle pressure on their tummies seems to help.

Pack them up and go for a ride. Try a stroller ride if the weather is nice or it is daytime. If not get in the car and take a leisurely drive. Leave the car radio off or put on soft music and enjoy the peace and quiet.

Let them cry. Some babies cry because they are over tired and no amount of rocking or singing to will calm them down. They also cry as a form of stress release. Let them release it in their crib. Stay near by and check on them to be sure they do not injure themselves. Do not leave them in there to cry for hours on end. Since endless crying can get to the best of us, allow them to "cry it out" alone long enough for you to calm down and collect yourself before picking them up. Be patient with them, they are only babies.

"If your newborn cries a lot, wrap him up. Most newborns feel cold or insecure with lose wrapping."
Sharla R, Mommy of Five, Kansas

Road Trip and Restaurant Activity
"Easy, simple and keeps them busy!"

Make necklaces by stringing beads, cut straws etc. onto yarn. For an edible twist use cheerios, pretzels, candies or dried fruit with a hole in the center. This can be worn to the grocery store to keep him/her busy counting the pieces or nibbling them off."

Trina T., Mommy of 2, NJ

Rudeness and Back Talk

When your child looks at you and speaks with a wickedness that has you convinced she is possessed, not only does your jaw drop from shock but also your neck hairs usually stand on end and you can feel yourself getting steamed. Resist the urge to strike back and try one of these suggestions.

R-E-S-P-E-C-T. Help your child learn the correct words to use in order to be more respectful in voicing her opinion. Many children do not know how to voice their unhappiness about situations.

Watch the tone. Tell your child up front that her tone of voice is disrespectful and not acceptable in your family. Once you have made this clear do not back down, make an appropriate punishment and stick to it.

Tell your child that you will talk with them when they have a nicer tone and then walk away from them.

Don't be rude or disrespectful back. They imitate every word and gesture.

Safety Gates

There are numerous uses for these gates. Here are a few.

Keep away. Use those child-safe interlocking gates to "pen" yourself and the grill away from little hands.

Do not enter. Enclose yourself and the ironing board in so you can be in the room with your children while getting some ironing done and they can play safely in your view.

Marking the territory. Safety pens are great for the "my side", "your side" dilemma. If they are the thick plastic colorful interlocking gates they can open up and stand alone to create low see through walls. These colorful partitions are a must for siblings who need their own space.

Save The Knees
Many knees of babies who crawl end up blackened and streaked by grass, dirt, sand and more. How do you protect these precious parts of babies not to mention the knee area of their clothes? Here is how one Dad put an end to dirty knees!

Cut the feet out of a pair of adult socks and pull the tubes over the baby's knees. You can fold them over once or twice depending on the size of your baby's knee and leg area. This will save both precious skin and pant leg alike.
Dave I., Daddy of Two, New Jersey

Sleeping Through The Night
Some babies sleep through the night from day one and others take much, much longer. How can you help this process along? Here are a few suggestions that may help. My son slept through the night by two and a half months and my daughter who is now nine months old only occasionally sleeps through with no rhyme or reason. So I am still experimenting with her. My pediatrician has told

me "All babies begin to sleep through the night at different ages so when she's ready she'll sleep through the night." Not what I wanted to hear but I smiled and thanked her anyway. Other moms had these tips.

Let them cry it out. I personally do not agree with this one. It pains me to hear little ones cry especially when it escalates to hyperventilation and sleeping from passing out or sheer exhaustion. How can they have a relaxing sleep if they went through the mill to get there?

Let them sleep with you. Do this only if you are comfortable with it. Some babies like companionship while they sleep. I only brought my daughter into bed with me if it was past 5 A.M. because I didn't want her to get into the habit of sleeping with me all night long. When I do let her in my bed she sleeps an extra 2 –3 hours. I'll take it.

Decrease the feedings and nighttime stimulation. If your baby is under 4 months old then it is more likely than not that she still requires round the clock feedings until her belly grows and can hold more foods. However if your baby is on solids and you are still feeding a bottle in the middle of the night, stop. Some babies get into the habit of a 2 am feeding even though they don't really need it. Begin decreasing the amount in the bottle and increasing the before bed feeding or wake them up for a feeding around 11:00 PM. When you have decreased their middle of the night bottle to two ounces replace it with water. If they don't enjoy it they might not bother waking up for it. Also do your diaper changes as quickly as possible and refrain from smiling and playing with your baby. This will help them to make a connection that when it is dark in the room we do not play and if we do not play why bother waking for it.

Try not to let them sleep the day away. If they are sleeping more than three or four hours during the day try to decrease their naptime. Once a schedule of napping is established you may find that your baby is taking a morning and an afternoon nap. Try not to let both total over three hours. Decrease one or both naps a little each day until three hours are achieved. Not all babies need three hours of nap a day and others may need more. Three hours just seems to be what most moms said worked for them. You'll have to experiment what will work for your baby. Don't short change yourself by having a tired cranky baby during the day just to get an extra hour of sleep at night – trust me it's not worth it.

Splashing in the Tub
Does tub time get your floor all wet? Try these Mom-tested tips out.

Get an inexpensive clear shower curtain and tension rod. Place it behind your fancy curtain. When the children are in the tub simply push back the nicer curtain and open up the clear one. That way you can see them and they can splash to their hearts content.

Take a clear shower curtain and fold it in half. Using four suction cups with hangers poke the metal hanger part through the curtain and stick it to the walls about half of the way down so you can still reach inside if you need to.

Spitting

This one is new to me but a mom wrote in with a tip and I figured if she dealt with it there might be someone else who could use a hint on how to stop it.

Have your child stand over a sink and spit continuously until they are finished spitting. Tell them that if they want to spit they are to do so in the sink only.

Stay in bed

OK, you just left your son's room after a story and kisses for the night and no sooner do you get down the stairs you hear the pitter patter of little feet. AAGGHHH! Besides strapping them down how do you get them to stay in there? Here are some helpful suggestions.

After tucking your little one in leave the room but wait outside the door a few feet away. As soon as he exits his room simply walk him back, re-tuck him in and kiss him goodnight. Give him no explanation, simply re-tuck give a kiss and tell him you love him and good night. Repeat this process each time he leaves his room as if it were the first. Do not show anger or agitation. Your child may be looking to get a rise out of you or think it is a game. If he gets no reaction the game is boring and he will stop. It will take a while, for me it took about 9 days but it did work. Each day there were fewer trips out than the night before until one day - nothing.

Present your child with three tickets. Make the tickets out of poster board or index cards. Each time she comes out she must give you a ticket when the tickets are gone she must stay in their room. If she comes out without a ticket they get one less the next night. Three tickets are just enough for the glass of water, bathroom and of course a kiss.

Change the environment. Some children feel lonely when left in their room and everyday sounds become magnified and scary. Try soft lullaby music so the sounds of the night while trying to fall asleep do not frighten them. Also a good ritual of checking for monsters under the bed and in closets doesn't hurt if your child requests it.

Tantrums

All is quiet in the store. You've almost made it to check out then suddenly it happens. The outburst begins. Over a seemingly innocent denial to a request for two choices of cookies instead of one your little one breaks out in the most horrendous tantrum of all time complete with kicking and flailing of the arms and legs. What do you do now?

A little prevention can go a long way. Before entering any store going over the rules and consequences with your child. Then stick to them. If you are going to purchase milk and apples tell your child "We are going into the store to buy one gallon of milk and some apples and nothing else. I expect you to mind your manners and ask for nothing extra. If you forget your manners there will be a time out when we get home, do you understand?" If the answer is no further clarification may be necessary. If the answer is yes then proceed into the store and buy only the milk and apples and leave. If all goes well in the store then praise your child for remembering her manners. If not follow through with a time out at home.

If an all out tantrum erupts you can choose to ignore it or deal with it. Ignoring the tantrum may work for some children, since they do not gain what they are fighting for they will give up. Ignoring a tantrum enough times will prove to them that this type of behavior does not work for getting what they want. Personally, I can't ignore a tantrum it goes straight to my last nerve. I tend to lean towards dealing with it.

Deal with the tantrum. Move as swiftly as possible to a quiet or less congested area of the store. Calmly tell your child that this type of behavior is unacceptable and if it continues you will leave the store immediately followed by a time out at home. Explain in a calm yet stern voice that the object so desired is not going to be purchased at this time. Continue to shop. If the tantrum continues then leave the store and use a time out at home followed by a discussion about the behavior. I have left many a store for this very reason. I find it better for my nerves as well as for my son's embarrassment since he dislikes people staring at him. That alone will fuel his tantrum to a higher elevation.

Get eye-to-eye with your child and count to ten in a calm voice. Try to get them to count a second set of ten along with you also in a calm voice. By the time they hit ten they just might be relaxed enough to talk about what is bothering them.

Teething Problems
Seeing those pearly whites pop through is a parents joy - finally more solid foods can be introduced. However, this joy is short lived due to the pain and discomfort it causes babies. Here are a few hints to help ease the pain.

For first teeth try freezing a carrot or banana and let they gnaw on it. It is cold enough to ease the pain and tasty enough to use often. Be sure to take the carrot or banana away once they are able to bite pieces off to prevent choking.

Dampen a washcloth and freeze it. Kids love to chew on these frozen pieces of cloth and they are safer than frozen foods.

Pops. An ice pop is also a fun and tasty treat for teething woes.

Toilet Paper Rollers
Children find unrolling the toilet paper extremely fun. However, when it is needed most, a lump of toilet paper on the floor is most annoying. Here is a great tip to stop them in their tracks.

Squash it. Before putting the roll on the spinner squash it so when they try to unroll it using the pull method they only get about 1 to 1 1/2 sheets.

Too Much Sugar
Between the cookies, cereals and juice that are out there not to mention the natural sugars in fruits and vegetables it is surprising that children nap at all. If you are concerned about the amount of sugar your child takes in here are a few hints to cut back without them knowing.

Slowly decrease the amount of juice they drink by diluting it with water. By the time you get to half and half they won't notice or miss the extra sweet stuff that is missing.

Buy unsweetened cereal and dress it up with sliced fruit.

Make snack time fun by adding fresh fruits and vegetables to the menu. Don't take the cookies away all at once. Delete one cookie and add a carrot or peach in its place. Let your kids make fruit kabobs instead of cookies or gummy fruit snacks. A little at a time is not as noticeable and makes transition easier.

"I just thought about this trick I did with my 2 and 3 year old after reading an article in Child's magazine about kids nowadays drinking to much juice. My son is always wanting juice, so to give him more opportunity to drink it I started to gradually every day take away a little juice and add a little water until eventually he now drinks half and half. He can't tell the difference anymore, and now I can give him a juice twice a day instead of only the once!!"

LaDonna E., Mommy of Two, Kentucky

Too Much TV

Pie eyes in front of a television set, though the quietness is music to a tired mom's ears, is not the best sport for children. Here are a few ways to cut down on the couch potato viewing time.

Be choosy. Predetermine the number of programs and the type of programs your child will watch and stick to it.

Interpret. Sit with your child while he watches a show to explain words, situations or to be comfort if something frightens him. You would be surprised at the amount of creepy things go on in seemingly innocent cartoons.

Find a healthy medium. Balance one hour of television to two hours of other activities.

Earn television time by doing chores. For instance feeding the pets, putting their toys away and putting their own clothes in their dresser earns them one approved show or tape.

Trying New Foods

This question will be on the lips of many moms trying to expand their child's one food menu. Here are three pretty good answers. The fourth one works better for babies and for taking medicine.

Keep offering it. Don't make a fuss if she won't try it at first. Simply keep adding it to the dinner/lunch plate over a period of time then give it a rest for a while and try again. Your child just might not be ready to try it. But persistence will pay off because on one night when you are not paying attention it will disappear from the plate and your dog won't be licking his chops. Some kids just need to take their time to try new things. If you harp on it or force them to eat everything on their plate you will gain nothing in your quest to get them to try anything new.

Have them take the "One Time Only" bite. Put a little on their plate and if they make a fuss ask them to take a "One Time Only " bite and if they do not like it then they can leave it on their plate. This way they will try it and if they like it they will eat it and if not they at least tried it. But do offer the food again at a later date in case their taste buds have changed.

Assign one point for each bite of the new food. Your child can redeem the points for something special like an extra bedtime story, a few extra minutes of playtime or something predetermined by you and your child.

Hide it in applesauce. Most babies as well as children love applesauce. Use it to camouflage other foods they normally would not eat alone. Also, applesauce is a good hider of icky medicines. This only works if it is in pill form, simply crush it up and put it in a spoon full of applesauce. If it is a liquid don't mix it with the applesauce because all you will have is icky applesauce. You can use the applesauce as a chaser. Give the medicine immediately followed by a spoonful of applesauce.

Whining

Nothing strikes a nerve quite like the sound of your child whining. Here are a few mom-tested ways of dealing with it.

Whining is somewhat like the tantrums. You can deal with it or ignore it. Some children work well by simply ignoring the whining talk and only respond to the pleasant voice. I myself have done this and found it to work. As soon as my son begins the whine I tell him once that I can only listen to his nice voice. After that if he continues to whine it goes unnoticed. I only respond to his nice voice.
Whine back. Allow your child to hear how silly or annoying it is. I have heard many moms tell me that their child would laugh at the silly whining of their moms and stop but when I tried it my son began to go into a tantrum. Needless to say I immediately stopped and went with the former suggestion of ignoring the whine and reinforcing the nice voice.

Check for allergies. One mom let me in on a secret that changed her life forever. Her son had allergies to certain food dyes and sugars. Once she cut back and eliminated them the whining and tantrums decreased measurably. *Always consult your doctor before changing your child's diet so as not to eliminate necessary vitamins and nutrients.

Ten Common Sense Tips For Raising Happier Children

In order to raise cheerful, contented and well-mannered children you will have to put in a lot of time and effort. If you repeat these ten tips each day you will be well on your way to raising healthy, happy and self-confident children.

1. Get physical! That's right you will need to get on all fours if necessary and play with your kids. Sitting on a park bench and watching your child climb, slide and run will not do. You must get up off your bottom and move. Not only will you and your child will have happier memories but also your child will feel he is important enough to play with. Your child wants someone to interact with so shake the sleep out of your jeans and go.

2. Don't plan every breath of their day. You know what it is like to have a full day of "things to do". You rush here and there barely slowing down for lunch and by the end of the day you collapse on the couch in exhaustion. Even if some of the items on your list were things you liked to do you didn't enjoy them because you were too rushed by the impending "list". Don't do this to your kids. Children need a break too. Make sure there is some down time during the day to just relax. Also, let them be in control of parts of the day. Their interests and your interests may not always be the same. You need to give and take during your together activities. There are going to be plenty of times when they will need to do things you want them to. Give in every now and then and do something they choose. Be flexible!

3. Relax together. Some children do not know how to relax. If you let them they will run and run until they pass out. This is not healthy. If you suspect your child does not know how to relax, which may be the case if they never see you taking a break, then show them. If they see how you relax whether it is reading a book, taking a nap or just sitting in the sun watching the clouds move overhead they may be inclined to do the same. If they only see you on the move they will feel the need to do the same.

4. Laugh a lot. Be silly. Believe it or not children have stress just like adults and the best way to alleviate it is to laugh. Children have a natural silliness to them so join in the fun. Don't be a grump. The point here is to have more happy memories than sad ones so break out the giggles. Remember you can't laugh and cry at the same time so if you have a choice - choose laughter. Not sure how to let loose? Here are a few examples: Make silly faces in a mirror together, have "tickle time", go outside and plant jelly beans, make animal sounds and try to guess the animals, play leap frog with stuffed animals, make a tent with a sheet and chairs and picnic in it, throw a birthday party for a stuffed animal, paint pictures with your noses.

5. Praise your child whenever possible. So often children are told what they are doing wrong they probably have a difficult time believing they can do anything right. We all fall into this trap. We say things like "Don't jump on the couch", "Don't swing that in the house", "Don't sing so loud", Don't, Don't, Don't. Of course we need to deter problems or dangerous behaviors but let's not lose sight of all the positive things your child does during the day. If you must discipline try not to use the word "don't" Not sure how? The next time your little one throws a ball in the house try saying this: "Wow, you threw that very far but ball throwing can be dangerous in the house so let's save it for when we play outside". Now, getting back to praise, be specific when you are telling your child he did something good. Mention the behavior you wish to reinforce this will help him remember what it is he did appropriately for instance, "Nicholas, you remembered your manners and said "Thank You" without my asking, I am very proud of you" or "You did a terrific job helping me to clean up these toys". If you forget to be specific in naming the action they are being praised for at least be creative in the positive words you use. If you hear the same thing over and over it tends to loose its sparkle. Kids know this as well. Need help with a few words of praise? Here are 50 ways to say Good Job.

Superb!
Great Job!
Excellent!
Wonderful!
I'm very proud of you.
You're very good at hat.
Nicely Done!
You learn fast!
Way To Go!
You figured that out quick!
That's the way to do it.
Sensational!
Keep it up!
You've got the hang of it
Good going.
That's really nice

Fantastic!
That's using your noodle!
Fabulous
I knew you could do it.
You picked it right up.
Congratulations!
Bravo!
You did that very well.
Amazing!
You are amazing.
That's the way!
Now you've got it.
Super!
Well done.
Terrific!
That's Right!

Sanity Savers For Frazzled Parents

That's Great!
Outstanding!
You remembered!
I like that
Good For You!
WOW!
Nice!
Marvelous!
Good thinking!
You are very clever.

You're on target.
Hooray!
You did it!
You are so smart.
Good job!
You figured it out.
That's thinking!
Fine job.
Nice one!

6. Don't expect perfection. Whether your child is 5 months or 5 years old they are still relatively new to this world and only been exposed to the proper way of completing many functions a small number of times. Their little minds, acting like sponges, are trying desperately to gather as much information as it possibly can to assimilate and perform many daily tasks. It will take many, many, many attempts at trying to complete a task a certain way before they accomplish it. And even at that the accomplishment will arrive with frayed edges. Be patient and treat each attempt as the first and you will take the pressure of perfection off of your little one whom so desperately wants to not only help you with grown up things but wants to do so many things on his own. Your child should be driven to please himself as far as accomplishing a task. Don't make him feel a failure when an attempt is not flawless. This will only make him less eager to try at all.

7. Feed your child right. A body uses food as fuel. If you fill it with junk food you will find that it doesn't run well. It may speed up and slow down throughout the day making the driver (your child) very grumpy. Make sure your child is not hungry. No fuel means no energy, which means a grumpy child. Keep snacks and meals as healthy as possible. I am not saying never allow your child a treat. By all means indulge them every now and then just use good judgment on when and how much. For example, If you give your child a sugary treat just before nap or bedtime good luck in getting them to rest at all let alone soundly. The same goes for mealtime foods. If your child has a sugary cereal with fruit for breakfast followed by a few cookies and juice for snack then a peanut butter and jelly sandwich (which alone has plenty of sugar), an apple and juice for lunch you might as well call Nassau for a countdown to lift off. Many foods have hidden sugars. Read labels and act accordingly.

8. Self-Expression. Give your child plenty of opportunities to express himself. Play various types of music and let him dance or color to it. I know the push is for classical music to stimulate brain function these days but don't rule out good old rock and roll, jazz, blues, country etc. Take your child to a museum and show him many different types of art from sculptures to paintings and more. Allow your child to be creative at home. Save as many empty rolls of paper towels, toilet paper, tissue boxes, egg cartons and cans with lids as possible. Break out the glue or string and create. Use clay or make papier-mâché to create masterpieces. Whatever seems to interest your child indulge him for as long as you can.

9. Teach them independence. Children want to do for themselves. Show them how, just remember "Common Sense Tip #6". If you do for them all the time they will never learn how to do for themselves. Allow your child the sense of pride that comes with doing something without asking for help. Every thing your child can do for himself gives him that much more control over his life. Don't worry he will always need you in his life but rather than his need for you to do for him he will need you to be there for him.

10. Listen to your child. There is nothing more demeaning than to talk to someone who is paying less than half attention to you. Don't make the newspaper or television more important than your child. Stop what you are doing, get on an eye-to-eye level and listen to what your child is saying. Whether it is about a pretend bear that came to his afternoon camp out or how he dug a huge hole in the sandbox or simply that he loves you, Listen, Listen and Listen. Not only should you look your child in the eye when he speaks to you but reply to your child so he knows you heard him.

Time Saving Tips

Everyone could use a few extra minutes in his or her day – especially parents. Here are a few tips that could add a little time here and there making daily tasks less stressful.

Prioritize. Make a list of what needs to get done the night before. Go through the list and determine what is important and what can wait. Start with the most important and work your way through the list. This way at the end of the day the most burdensome tasks have been taken care of and the rest can get accomplished when time permits leaving you to breathe a little easier.

When preparing your meals make twice as much. Freeze the second portion to use at a later date. This works well when you run out of time to prepare from scratch, simply defrost and heat.

Prepare large amounts of chopped onions, peppers, parsley or other ingredients you tend to use often and freeze. When preparing the meal take them out and add to the recipe. This does not seem like a lot but every few minutes here and there adds up.

Prepare meals the night before. Breakfast lunches and dinner can be made the night before then frozen until needed.

When making pancakes don't throw out remaining batter. Simply make as many pancakes as you can with what's left and put in the fridge or freezer. When you or our children want pancakes voila! By the way, they are cheaper than the store bought pre-made ones.

Put a sturdy laundry basket in the trunk of your car or back of your van the next time you go grocery shopping. When you load up from the cart to car simply place them in the basket. When you get home all you need to do is carry up one basket with maybe a second trip to do the job. Otherwise you usually need 4 – 5 trips while stringing bags up your arm keeping you off balance and exhausted.

While the kids are in the tub clean the toilet and sink. Hey, you have to be in there anyway.

Clean while you cook. If you put spices away after using them and clean up used pots and pans while cooking then you will have less to clean after the meal cutting your after dinner clean up time in half.

Planning. If you have many errands to run plan your route so you do not backtrack. When planning your route make your first stop the furthest destination on your list so when the errands are done the ride home is quick.

Avoid going out between 11 am and 1 pm. This will help you to avoid longer lines in stores and congested streets due to all those people trying to run their errands at lunchtime. Another good time to avoid is between 4 pm and 6 pm, rush hour. Rush Hour - need I say more?

Be a cheapskate. Purchase an inexpensive garage sale vacuum cleaner and leave it on your second floor so when it comes time to clean up there you do not have to lug the vacuum cleaner up the stairs, saving you time and energy.

Keep your cleaning things in a bucket so you don't have to make unnecessary trips to your linen closet. This helps for ease of carrying them to a second floor as well. If you choose, keep a second set of cleaning supplies in a bucket on the second floor so you don't have to run downstairs to get your supplies.

Put your bed linens in under the bed storage boxes under their respective beds so you don't waste time in your linen closet searching for the right bed sheets for the right bed. This will also help your kids to help you by giving them the opportunity to make their own bed. They simply strip their beds, something they can all do, and pull out a clean set of linens from the box under their bed and have at it. It may not be perfect but with a handful of tries they'll get it.

Avoid wrinkles. I don't know about you but I hate to iron. One of the better things cleaning and laundry companies came up with are those wrinkle releasers. Take the clothing out of the dryer as soon as it stops so you have fewer wrinkles then follow the directions on the squirt bottle – it really does work.

Money Saving Tips

Who couldn't use a little extra cash? Here are a few helpful tips on saving money wherever possible.

Consignment shops. Buy and sell your children's clothes here. You can really find some great prices on good clothes for your kids for both play and party. Selling gently used outgrown or never worn clothing at a consignment shop is a great way to earn a little extra cash as well.

Coupons. Clip, clip, clip. You can find them in the Sunday paper, magazines, through coupon clubs, the courtesy counter of your local food store and more. If you use them at your store and they double them – bonus!

Make homemade cards. Since the average card costs about $2.00 and it is more or less read and enjoyed for a few days before it meets an early demise make them from the heart. Get out the paper, markers, stickers and such and have at it. A homemade card is not only treasured longer it costs about 1/10th the price of a store-bought one. Think about it, if you make one card a month at the cost of 25cents each you spent $3 as opposed to $24 with store bought.

Homemade postcards. If you do get store bought cards cut off the top and use the pictured half as a postcard. Postage is cheaper than a letter and the postcard was free. Check with your post office for size restrictions on postcards.

Use the library. Instead of renting a movie from the video store go to your local library and check you their selection. If you do not have a good selection there start a borrower's group in your neighborhood or family.

Make homemade wipes. Using a 10-Cup bowl with lid mix 2 cups water, 2 Tbl baby wash and 2 Tbl baby oil. Cut a roll of paper-towels in half and remove the center cardboard tube then immerse in the solution.

Take your home made wipe solution and put it in a squirt bottle. Squirt the solution on a piece of paper towel or directly on your baby's skin and wipe with cloth or tissue.

Make those hose last longer and buy fewer. Wet a pair of pantyhose and place in a baggie. Freeze in the freezer. Before you need to wear them defrost them at room temperature. They will run less.

Make household cleaners. Great all purpose cleaner – mix ½ cup of ammonia with 1/3 cup white vinegar, ¼ cup baking soda and 1 gallon of warm water.

Don't throw out the broth! The next time you boil chicken either for the grill or to make soup save some of the broth and freeze in ice-cube trays or empty applesauce cups. A great way to add chicken broth/flavor to your home cooked recipes without all the sodium found in store bought brands – not to mention it is free.

Join the club. If you do not have coupon clubs in your area then start one and trade what you don't need for what you do. If you choose not to start one then ask your friends or family members who do not clip to save their unwanted coupon pages for you.

Put an apple in a bag of potatoes to keep them from sprouting or wrinkling for up to 8 weeks.

Save your dry cleaning bags and use them for trash bags. Simply tie them in a knot at the end, insert it into your trash container and have at it.

Blackout! During hot sunny days close your curtains to deflect direct sunlight to help keep your house cool. This little bit will help to keep cooling costs down.

Hang sheets and blankets out to dry in the sun. They take longer in a dryer costing you valuable dollars in electricity. Besides the money saving point they will smell great.

Don't buy wrapping paper. Use comic strip paper from Sunday's Newspaper to wrap children and adult gifts. You can also use unused wallpaper. If you choose a brown paper bag could do nicely with a few stickers or twine for a rustic look.

Cover your child's schoolbooks with brown grocery bags. Simply cut them open and turn the over, fold the top and bottom up and insert the cover flaps. Your child can decorate them with markers, stickers or leave plain.

Do your grocery shopping alone. When you bring the kids or your spouse or even both – yikes! – You tend to spend more money.

Go to school. Need your nails done? How about a trim? If you have a vocational school near you take advantage of hidden savings. These schools are always looking for people to practice on. They are very good at what they do – they do not let their students work on people unless they are ready so you will get good service and they charge considerably less than a salon.

Go to school. Does your car need a tune-up, small repair or even a paint job? Once again try your local vocational/trade schools. You get a job well done at a great price.

Pay more! This one won't sound like a money saver but it is. Pay extra on your mortgage each month and apply it directly to the principle. This will knock several years off of your mortgage and save you thousands in interest.

Purchase a pump to put liquid soap in mixed with water. This makes nice foam and doesn't get wasted like straight liquid that slips off your hands and down the drain. I've purchased mine through a Pampered Chef demonstration but I am sure they can be found elsewhere.

Use an inexpensive shampoo instead of those liquid body wash soaps. You spend less and get more this way.

Save with every flush. Put a brick wrapped in a plastic bag or a filled water jug in your toilet tank. This will help cut the water that is flushed away saving on your water usage bill.

Don't throw out the junk mail. Go through your junk mail and pull out the return envelopes. You can easily put your own labels for recipient and sender over the pre-printed ones and voila you now have a useful envelope.

Save the diapers! When your child outgrows their diaper size and you are stuck with leftovers simply open them up and attach them to your swiffer-type mop and go. They work great.

Don't get burned. Put meats in cheap plastic bags, store bags found in the fruit and veggies section or the bags that hold your groceries. Insert these cheaper bagged meat items in a good freezer bag. Make sure your items are marked with a label or tag on the cheap bag. Doing this will keep your meat from getting freezer burn as well as provide you with a re-usable good freezer bag since the meat never touches the good quality bag.

"Garage sale for the sizes you need ahead. It saves tons of money."

Sharla R, Mommy of Five, Kansas

Household Tips

Here are some pretty neat "tricks" for cleaning and freshening your home. Some are quite interesting and may sound silly but they do work so give them a try.

The following tips will help you out with some unexpected yet inevitable household mishaps.

Crayon on walls. To remove young artists crayon work from your walls try making a paste out of baking soda and water. Using a sponge rub the mixture over the crayon markings until they are gone. They do come off with a little effort and elbow grease.

Gum in carpet. Gum sticking to your carpet? Freeze the gum with an ice cube then break it into pieces with a blunt object, a meat mallet works well. Then simply vacuum the pieces away. If a residue remains then apply either club soda or a carpet cleaner to the area and blot. If you do use a store bought carpet cleaner be sure to perform the spot test first.

Hairspray on painted walls. Where you a little overzealous with the hairspray in the bathroom? If you have painted walls try one of these remedies.
1. Mix 1 part shampoo with 4 parts water in a squirt bottle.
2. Mix a little white vinegar with water in a squirt bottle. Spray and wipe – all gone.

In the laundry

Ring around the collar. Mix 1 part shampoo with 3 parts water in a spray bottle. Spray on the stain and let sit for 3 – 5 minutes then launder as usual.

Sour or musty smelling dishtowels and potholders. Wash with laundry detergent and ½ cup baking soda.

Ink stains on clothing. Hairspray the ink stain before laundering.

Blood Stains on clothes. Pour a little peroxide on a clean cloth and wipe off the stain.

Kitchen and Bathroom

Grimy kitchen floor. Mix 1 cup of white vinegar with 2 gallons of water and wash well.

Stinky Sink. Pour 1 cup of white vinegar followed by 1 cup of baking soda down the drain flush with very hot water

Clogged Sink. Drop three Alka Seltzer tablets down the drain followed by one cup of white vinegar. Wait a few minutes, and run the hot water

Refrigerator or Freezer odor. Place an open box of baking soda inside and change every few months.

Mineral deposits on faucets and showerhead. Use a spray bottle of white vinegar. Spray the faucets or showerheads, let sit approx. 3 minutes then wipe. Repeat if necessary.

Toilet Stains. Drop in two to three Alka Seltzer Tablets into the toilet. Wait about 20 minutes and then simply brush and flush.

Permanent Marker Stains on Counter Top (example: store receipt blue ink). Dab some rubbing alcohol on paper towel and rub away that ink.

Smelly kitchen sponge. Either replace with a new one or microwave the smelly one on full power for 1 minute – this kills the bacteria.

Microwave Odors. Slice a fresh lemon and place in a glass microwave safe bowl with enough water to float the slices. Microwave on high power for 5 – 10 minutes or until your microwave is nice and steamy.

Microwave gunk buildup. Microwave a bowl of water for a 1-3 minutes and then let it sit 10 minutes. The inside gets very moist and everything wipes away easily.

Tupperware smells icky. Fill the Tupperware with water and add 1 teaspoon of vanilla. Let it sit overnight then wash.

Pesky plastic bags. Are empty plastic grocery bags taking over? Save an empty tissue box to stuff these bags in. The boxes hold a lot and give you the opportunity to pull out one at a time.

Spots on Stainless steel. will disappear with this tip. Soak the pot or pan in powder detergent - Cascade works wonders – and a little liquid dish soap in HOT water for a few hours to overnight. Wash as you normally would and the spots are gone.

Ginger C., Mommy of Two, NJ

Other Cleaners

Window cleaner. Mix ½ cup of white vinegar with 1 gallon of warm water. Cleaning Tip: Use vertical strokes when washing the outside of windows and horizontal on the inside. Doing this will help you to tell which side has the streaks.

Rug or carpet stain remover. Club soda – what else?

Great all-purpose cleaner. Mix a solution of ½ cup ammonia, 1/3 cup white vinegar, and ¼ cup baking soda with 1 gallon of warm water.

Jewelry Cleaner. Get out an old toothbrush and polish them with toothpaste. Or drop two Alka Seltzer tablets into a glass of water and submerge the jewelry for two minutes.

Build-up at the bottom of your Glass Vase. Fill the vase with water. Drop in two Alka Seltzer Tablets and let them do all the work.

Longer Lasting Candles. Place your candles in the freezer for at least 3 hours prior to burning.

Cleaning those Artificial Floral Arrangements. To clean artificial flowers, pour some salt into a paper bag and add the flowers. Shake vigorously and the salt will absorb all of the dust and dirt leaving your artificial flowers looking like new!

Uses for baby wipes other than the baby.
Wiping fingerprints from walls

Dusting
Wiping up spots on the kitchen floor
Wiping up drips of formula from a bottle on the carpet

Uses for fabric softener sheets other than in the dryer
Hang in closet for freshness
Place in drawers
Place one under the seat of your car
Place one at the bottom of wastebaskets or laundry hamper for a fresh smell.
Put them in shoes or sneakers overnight to eliminate smells by morning.
Eliminate static electricity from your television or computer screen. Wipe the screens with a used dryer sheet to deter dust from resettling as quickly.

Tips for a fresh smelling home
Clean with the windows open.
Use Febreze on sofas, carpets, pet beds etc. (Read label directions before use)
Simmer cinnamon sticks and either sliced orange or lemon with water on your stovetop.
Plants, plants and more plants. Plants take in carbon dioxide and give off oxygen. The larger the leaf the more stale air is processed into clean air.

Miscellaneous
Don't get tangled in Cords. Tuck appliance cords in empty toilet paper rolls. It will keep them neat, tangle free and you can write on the roll what appliance it belongs to. If a paper roll has you concerned for fires then use cut PVC tubes instead.

Need to unseal an envelope? Put the wrong check in the wrong envelope? Forget to sign the check? Or better yet, forget to put it in the envelope before you sealed it? Simply put the envelope in the freezer for a few hours, and then slide a knife under the flap. Correct your mistake and reseal the envelope.

Tips for Getting Things Done Around The House

There are ways in which you can accomplish a few things so you do not find yourself living in a clutter filled filthy home with nothing clean to wear but what you were dressed in the last time you got caught out in the rain.

First of all enlist some help. I don't mean hire a maid and a cook, unless you are financially able to do so. Children are great helpers. Now don't expect perfection. If you do then hire out otherwise get your cleaning supplies your child/children and get started. Even a child as young as one can help straiten up the house, do laundry and even help prepare a meal. You don't think so? Think again.

Dusting the House

Give your child a clean dust cloth. Spray the cleaner and start wiping. Children love to imitate and follow along. Put on a little music and they will dance and dust with you.

Make dust eater puppets out of old socks. Simply put an old sock on yours and your child's hand and feed the hungry dust puppet with his favorite food – dust. The dirtier the puppet is the happier his tummy is. Kids love to feed hungry dust puppets.

Straightening up the House

Play the "I have cleaned it" game. What you need is a messy room and helping hands. Get down and start cleaning while singing the following song to the tune Pop Goes the Weasel - All around the room today I see that things are messy, when I pick them up off the floor POP I have cleaned it! You can even jump on the word POP to make it more fun. Keep singing until the room is tidy.

Get small baskets or dishpans and assign them to each member of your household. As you see things out of place put it in the right container and let each individual bring his or her container to their room.

If you have steps and choose not to use containers as in the tip above, assign each member of your household a step and place items that belong to them on the appropriate step for taking up as they go.

Play musical clean up. Play music and everybody starts cleaning. When the music stops they are to freeze in a silly pose. Keep it up until the room is clean.

Laundry

Let kids help with folding. Kids may not make the best folders but they try hard. When my son was two, I taught him how to help me fold washcloths. They weren't the neatest but they were folded, sort of. He would then help me put them away. He was so proud of his work. I was very pleased to see him admire his work that I fought off my desire to re-fold his attempts and let them stay just the way he made them. Now he helps me with towels and shirts and pants. Socks are great to give to a 6+-month-old child; they are kept occupied with these new found toys giving you the opportunity to fold other items.

Play a color sort game. When sorting laundry for washing have the kids help sort them out by playing a color game. Assign each child a color to find and put in a pile. Before you know it you are sorted and ready to wash.

Provide children with their own basket. As you fold the clothes place them in appropriate baskets. Each child will then take their own laundry to their rooms and put them away. Don't stress over perfection when they put them in drawers, remember it is all about process. For younger children help may be required. Another tip is to put their pictures on the baskets for easy identification.

If you prefer not to have the kids help out then keep your laundry folding to sheets, towels, and whites. These things can stay in baskets or the dryer for a while until you can get to them and they don't require ironing.

In the Kitchen

Time to make dinner? If the meal is complicated or has many parts do as much of your prep work as possible during the children's naptime. That way you can simply pop the pre-arranged meals into the oven when needed. However, kids can make an awesome salad if given the chance. They can tear pieces of lettuce and add pre-cut cucumbers, carrots and tomatoes into the salad bowl. I like to make salad in a plastic bowl that has a lid so when all of the ingredients are in I simply seal it up and let my son shake it for a nice tossed salad. Kids can also help with the main course. You will probably not see a more tenderized piece of meat than that of one fixed by a three year old. Wrap your meat in wax paper for sanitary reasons and let your child have at it with a meat mallet. This is a great way for them to get out aggressions without hurting anyone. Let them pour and mix. This is a great way to teach math. Yes math. They can count the number of cups or teaspoons of ingredients that are needed to put into the bowl. They can also count the number of times they stirred the ingredients together. They can even count the number of ingredients used to make dinner. Guess what? Counting is math! Children can also set the table. They can set one plate out for each person, one napkin for each person and so forth. Hmm this sounds like one to one correspondence to me. HA - math again! So break out the measuring spoons/cups and make some cookies and tell your husband you taught a math lesson today!

Make your little one feel independent in the kitchen. Clean out one cupboard cabinet to store child safe items such as plastic containers, empty food boxes, pots and pans etc. This can keep young children quite happy for a while as you prepare meals and snacks. For older children clean out the lower shelf of the fridge to store safe snack items they can get for themselves. Duplicate this in the pantry to store snack and breakfast items. Little ones feel so "Big" when they can make choices for themselves and get things on their own.

Stuff around the house

No matter what type of toy shelf, box or storage facility you have come up with for your children's play things it is inevitable that you will find them scattered throughout your home. This also goes for articles of clothing taken off and dropped wherever. Here are a few tips that may help fight off the need to grab a garbage bag and fill it up.

Again, a small box, dishpans or laundry baskets with each family members name on it is a great way to go. As you see it on the floor, grab it and toss it into the appropriate bin. At the end of the day each person is to take his/her bin to his or her room and put it away. Empty bins are to be brought out the next day for refills.

If you do not wish to fill boxes or baskets and you have a staircase, assign one step to each person and plop the items that go up on the appropriate step. When they go up so should their stuff.

A final thought about housework and children: If you put more value on your children's happiness and learning than on the appearance of your home you will be well on your way to raising happy, healthy, confident, and self-reliant children.

All About Toys

Definition of a Toy and their Purpose

First of all I would like to define what toys are and what
they can accomplish. At this moment you are probably
thinking - "I know what a toy is and what it does, you
purchase it from the store, put batteries in it and it will
amuse my child for hours." Let me begin by explaining
that a toy is <u>any object</u> that a child investigates and
manipulates in a variety of ways. I tend to favor the
"homemade" toys over the ones you purchase at a store
for a few reasons. First and foremost, toys that have one
function (i.e. they give the same response over and over)
do not allow the child to use his imagination. There is not
much investigation and exploration that comes from
manipulating a toy of this nature. Second, Toys with a
number of things such as lights, sounds and movement
happening at once can be overwhelming and over
stimulating to a young child to the point that the child
shuts himself down from the toy and rarely explores it.

Furthermore, toys are more than simple tools for
entertainment; they provide a child with an outlet for self-
expression as well as a tool for fostering developmental
growth. I bet you are now wondering what skills a toy
can develop. Just for you, I have listed and defined each
of these "developmental skills" followed by some toys
that foster them. These toys can be purchased or
homemade. Don't underestimate the homemade ones!

<u>Fine Motor Skills</u>: Movement and coordination of the
hands and fingers. <u>Toys</u>: Blocks, boxes and containers,
puzzles, books or magazines, play dough, all craft
supplies, instruments (purchased or homemade), sand and
sandbox toys.

Gross Motor Skills: Movement and coordination of the arms, legs and body. Toys: Push, pull and ride on toys, balls and bubbles.

Sensory Exploration: Stimulation of the five senses; taste, touch, hearing, sight and sound. Toys: Push, pull and ride on toys, blocks, boxes and containers, puzzles, balls, books, magazines, play dough, bubbles, all craft supplies, instruments (purchased or homemade), dress up clothes, sand and sandbox toys.

Pre-Math Skills: Spatial recognition, shape, color and one to one correspondence. Toys: Blocks, boxes and containers, puzzles, books, magazines, play dough and instruments (purchased or homemade).

Language Skills: Formulation of speech and speech patterns from single words to phrases and sentences. Toys: Push, pull and ride on toys, blocks, boxes and containers, puzzles, balls, books, magazines, play dough, bubbles, all craft supplies, instruments (purchased or homemade), dress up clothes, sand and sandbox toys.

Imagination Skills: Ability to use representational reasoning using concrete or non-tangible objects. For example: A child uses salad tongs as a "construction crane" to move "pipes", blocks, around the job site, his play room, while shouting commands to his workers, plastic dinosaurs. It can even be something as simple as using a box as a house or a laundry basket as a car. Toys: Push, pull and ride on toys, blocks, boxes and containers, balls, books, magazines, play dough, bubbles, all craft supplies, instruments (purchased or homemade), dress up clothes, sand and sandbox toys.

<u>Creativity</u>: Ability to use various objects in a way other than they were originally intended. <u>Toys</u>: Push, pull and ride on toys, blocks, boxes and containers, puzzles, balls, books, magazines, play dough, bubbles, all craft supplies, instruments (purchased or homemade), dress up clothes, sand and sandbox toys.

When it comes to toys remember less is more. Look no further than your kitchen cabinets or closets to find great, safe toys for children of all ages. Here are a few "homemade" toys and their manufactured counterpart.

Plastic Measuring Cup = Nesting Blocks

Empty Boxes and Containers = Blocks

Wooden Spoon and Pot or Plastic Bowl = Drum

Two Pan Lids = Symbols

One Sheet and Two Chairs = A Tent

Sock or Paper Bag Puppet = Popular Puppets

Paper Cups, Plates and Pitcher = Tea Set

Old Clothing and Shoes = Dress Up Clothes

Empty Box decorated by kids and lined with a small blanket = Cradle for Baby Doll

Large Empty Handbag with a Shoulder Strap and Junk Mail = Postal Carrier Bag

Toy Storage Tips

If you have an infant then chances are good that you probably haven't accumulated enough toys yet to make their presence a consideration. Rest assured that by the time a few holidays and their first birthday have passed you will be struggling with the same dilemma that faces every parent. What will we do with all these toys?

There are many ways toys can be stored. Here are some common storage solutions as well as some unique ways of handling the mountain of toys.

Open Shelves let you see each toy and they provide easy access to them. They do however, pose the threat of tumbling over when pulled or climbed on. They also don't work well when storing items that have many little parts. You will need many shelves and plenty of wall space if you have amassed a good amount of toys in your home. If you do go with shelves then I suggest you secure them to the walls with furniture straps. You can find these inexpensive straps where most safety products are sold.

Commercial Toy Boxes are something of a space saver since you don't need as many toy boxes as you would shelves for the same amount of toys. They do keep toys out of sight making for a neat looking room however, toys tend to break when they are thrown in a box with other toys piled on top of them and pushed down with a lid. It is a simple fact of life that the toy your child wants to play with is usually the one at the bottom of the box. The child's process for finding this toy is to hurl all other toys backwards over their head without concern for the well being of these toys or anyone in their way. The result of this quest is a messy room and more broken toys. Not to mention the lids on some of these toy boxes can be unsafe for young children. Some of these lids are made of heavy wood and can come crashing down on a child bent over the side searching for a toy. Hinges are another hazard. Little fingers are fascinated with metallic objects and when the desire to touch takes over their bodies and they stick these little fingers where they shouldn't be – pinch! To avoid the lid and hinge problem some people have tried to use oversized plastic storage boxes. Not a bad idea but you still have the favorite toy at the bottom and the crushed toy problem. If you do have a toy box and choose not to use it for toys, you can use it to store seasonal items (clothing, toys, videos, decorations), extra blankets and pillows or your overflow of stuffed animals. If it is to be kept in your child's room install a lock to keep your child safe.

Boxes, Boxes, Boxes. Gather up your old boxes from shoebox size to television size and all in between. Glue or secure together with packaging tape. Cover the outsides with contact paper and there you have it, homemade shelves. You don't need to cover the outside with contact paper. You can let your child decorate the outside with markers or stickers. Old wipe containers are good for storing little pieces.

Storage Containers. Use varying size of storage containers. My son sorts (well sometimes) his toys into the shoebox size containers (i.e. one for cars, pegs, small wooden blocks, dinosaurs, etc.) a helpful hint is to have a picture of the object that is to be placed in the box taped to the outside of it. This hint will help your little one to sort these small items with little or no help from you. The larger containers hold larger toys and groups of toys such as tools and construction gear for one box and large blocks in another.

Shoe Holders. Are small toys getting underfoot? Try hanging a clear shoe holder on your child's door. It is great for small toys, hair accessories, beanie toys or craft supplies.

Old Dresser Drawers. Attach wheels to old dresser drawers and fill with small toys. These drawers full of treasures can easily slide under a bed. Two can fit under a single bed.

Laundry Baskets. Here is another way to go. They are not too expensive and they can hold a lot of toys. They come in many colors, which makes for easy room coordination.

Toy Rotation. If the toys are still taking over your home try this. Take a box and fill it with some toys and put them in a closet. In a few weeks time bring them out and put away another box full. You will be surprised at how your child will treat this old toy as if it were brand new.

Toy Sale. If you find that your child still doesn't play with it put it aside to donate to a local group i.e. church, shelter or day care center or for a garage sale. If you do sell them at a garage sale let your child use the money to purchase a new toy. This works well and weeds out what is not used. Not to mention your child's old toy can bring new joy to someone else.

Save those plastic bags that your comforter sets come in to store toys.

Recycle toys with friends or cousins. If your toys are still in good condition but are not played with often then trade with some friends or cousins for a fresh set of toys to play with.

Milk crates make good toy holders. These are especially good for outside storage of sand toys.

Chapter 3
Time To Eat

Making a breakfast, snack or lunch that will please our most picky eaters is always challenging. Not only do you want to please everyone but also you want to make each meal as nutritional as possible. I am presenting to you a handful of kid tested breakfast, snack and lunch recipes that are relatively simple to make, reasonably nutritious and very tasty.

Breakfast

Is your morning harried by the battle over breakfast? Maybe you don't have time to cook big morning meals or maybe your kids aren't interested in what is on the menu. Now you can give your kids something different that is not only nutritious but also delicious, it is easy with these recipes.

<u>Toasty Treats</u>
Slice of bread or English muffin
Jelly or butter
Fresh or canned fruit cut into slices, wedges or chunks

Toast your bread or English muffin and spread with either jelly or butter. Arrange on a plate with fruit pieces to resemble a face, car, teddy bear etc... If you are using toast simply cut a shape using cookie cutters and decorate from there. Be creative.

Nested Egg
Slice of bread
Egg

Using a circle or flower cookie cutter punch out the center of a piece of bread. Put butter in a skillet and lightly toast the bread on both sides. Crack an egg and pour it into the center of the toast and cook until done. If you prefer, you can scramble the egg before pouring it into the cut out of the toast.

Nibblers
½ cup of yogurt
1 cup of granola
Apple, banana, pineapple chunks

Place a toothpick in the fruit and let your kids dip the fruit in the yogurt and coat with granola. These nibblers are very tasty. These are also great frozen.
*Note: Only use toothpicks with children 3 and older.

Yogurt Surprise
Plain yogurt
Nuts (sunflower seeds, walnuts etc.)
Granola
Honey
Fresh fruit cut into pieces

Let your child create his own flavor. Let him mix nuts, granola, honey and/or fruit into plain yogurt for a tasty surprise.

Shakes
If your child is not a breakfast eater here are two great shake recipes that are sure to please.

Monkey Business
Banana
1 Cup of milk
Food Coloring

In a blender mix one banana with 1 cup of milk. Mix in a drop or two of your favorite food coloring for an eye-catching sight and serve.

Fruity Cow
1 Cup of milk
Assorted fruits (strawberry, banana, grapes, kiwi etc.)

In a blender mix 1 cup of milk with an array of your favorite fruits. Enjoy!

Hint: Add granola or nuts for the crunch factor.

Snacks

Whether it is a quick snack on the go or a sit down create a snack time with your child these are fun to make and eat.

The Right Mix
3 Cups of assorted cereal
¼ Cup raisins   ¼ Cup nuts
¼ Cup pretzels   ¼ Cup sunflower seeds
4 oz. Chocolate (white or dark) – optional

Mix the above ingredients together in a bowl. By itself it is a great snack but to jazz it up a bit melt the chocolate and stir into the mix. Stir until the mix is well coated with chocolate. Chill. Enjoy!

Ocean Adventure
White frosting or Cream Cheese
Goldfish crackers
Blue food coloring   Graham crackers

Mix the blue food coloring with the frosting or cream cheese to represent "water". Spread the "water" on a graham cracker. Stick goldfish on top for an underwater snack.

Butterflies
Small curved pretzels
Small stick pretzels
Peanut Butter

Dip the flat edges of curved pretzels in peanut butter and stick one on each side of a thin pretzel. For a variation: Spread peanut butter in the cavity of a washed celery stalk and stick the curved pretzels in the peanut butter for wings.

Ants on an Apple
Apple slices   Peanut butter
Raisins
Spread peanut butter on each apple slice and add raisins.

Apple smiles
Apple slices   mini marshmallows
Peanut butter

Spread peanut butter on both apple slices. Place a few marshmallows side by side on the peanut butter side of one of the apple slices. Place the second apple slice, peanut butter side down, on top of the marshmallows.

Fish Bowl
Blue Jello
Gummy fish
Plastic cups

Make blue jello according to package instructions. Fill plastic cups with the jello. As it begins to harden, place gummy fish in the jello.

Summer Smoothies
8 ounces Milk 8 ounces Yogurt
Ice cubes   Fresh fruit cut into small pieces

Place the above ingredients into a blender and blend until smooth. Note: You can omit the milk and yogurt and add fruit juice instead.

Easy Cina-Cakes
½ c melted Butter   ½ c Sugar
1 tsp Cinnamon   10 refrigerator biscuits

Mix the melted butter, sugar and cinnamon together in a bowl. Place the biscuits in a round cake pan (all sides touching) and spread the mixture atop the biscuits. Bake as package directions indicate or until golden brown.

Lunch

Getting your kids to stop playing and eat lunch is trouble enough. Use these recipes to make lunch interesting and fun enough to sit down and take time out for.

Apple Sandwiches
1 Apple
Slices of Cheese
Slices of lunchmeat

Core and cut an apple into eight wedges. Put cheese and meat slices on top of one apple wedge and place another apple wedge on top.

Petite Calzones
1 c Ricotta   ¼ c grated Parmesan
½ c Grated Mozzarella
2 pkgs. Large Refrigerator Biscuits
1 Pepperoni stick, thinly sliced or thinly sliced ham

Mix the 3 cheeses together. Halve each biscuit horizontally and shape into an oval. Place the pepperoni or ham slice on first and then top with 1 tablespoon of the cheese mixture. Moisten edges with water, fold over and seal. Bake on greased cookie sheet at 350 degrees for approximately 20 min. Cool and enjoy. These are great alone or dipped in your favorite pasta sauce.

Tuna Face

Tuna fish prepared to taste
½ Breakfast muffin
Olives
Carrot shavings

Celery chunks
Cherry Tomatoes

Prepare tuna fish to your taste specifications. Spread on one half of a toasted breakfast muffin. Use two olives for eyes, a cherry tomato for a nose, carrot shavings for hair and celery chunks for the mouth.

Pigs in a blanket

Hotdogs cut into thirds
Ready to bake biscuits

Flatten each ready to bake biscuit with your hand. Roll each biscuit around one piece of hotdog and pinch the dough together so it doesn't come apart. Bake in the oven according to biscuit package directions. Serve with carrots, chips or french-fries. If choking is a concern simply cut the hotdogs further to create a flat side.

Shapewiches

Bread
Sandwich fillings
Cookie cutters

Add pizzazz to your old sandwiches. Make a nutritious sandwich from cold cuts or PB&J. Instead of simply cutting the crusts off the sandwiches make fun shapes out of them with cookie cutters.

Roll-Ups

Deli Meats and Cheeses
Carrot or Celery Sticks
Apple wedges

Peanut Butter (optional)

Simply roll up any combination of deli meats and cheeses. Place four of them on a plate in a square. Inside the meat square make a carrot square and then a celery square. In the very center place some apple wedges or a dollop of peanut butter for dipping. Variation: Roll the carrot sticks and celery sticks inside the deli meats for a crunchy surprise!

The Shredded Sandwich

Pita Bread
Sliced Olives
Shredded Carrots
Shredded Lettuce
Chopped or Shredded Deli Meats

Place a pile of shredded lettuce, carrots, olives and chopped deli meats on separate paper plates. Provide your child with a pita pocket and let them fill it to their hearts content. Enjoy.

Pizza-Noodle Roll

Pizza Dough
Chopped Ham and Pepperoni
Mozzarella Cheese
Cooked Noodles
Sauce (either homemade or store bought)

Roll out the pizza dough. Spread a layer of sauce on the dough. Mix a little sauce with the cooked noodles so they do not stick together. Sprinkle the ham, pepperoni, cooked noodles and mozzarella on top. Roll the pizza dough into a loaf shape and bake according to package directions. When cool cut into slices and serve with a dollop of sauce for dipping.

Cooking Quandaries

Here are a few tips to help out around the kitchen. Try them – they work.

Ice Cream Cone Drips
Stuff a miniature marshmallow in the bottom of a sugar cone to prevent those messy ice cream drips.

Perfect Pancakes
To get perfectly shaped pancakes every time you cook use a meat baster to "squeeze" your pancake batter onto the hot skillet/griddle.

No Buds on your Spuds
To keep your potatoes from budding, place an apple in the bag with the potatoes.

Don't crack under boiling water
To prevent your hard-boiled eggs from cracking, add a pinch of salt to the water before hard-boiling.

Sticky Treat Making
Run your hands under cold water before pressing Rice Krispie Treats in the pan and the marshmallow won't stick to your fingers.

Or
Use a piece of wax paper under your hand to press the Rice Krispie Treats in the pan.

The Juiciest Juices
To get the most juice out of fresh lemons and oranges, bring them to room temperature and roll them under your palm against the kitchen counter before squeezing.

Removing burnt food from pans
Add a drop or two of dish soap and enough water to cover bottom of pan. Bring to a boil on stovetop. When cool wash as usual.

Pre-Treat your Tupperware to prevent stains
Spray your Tupperware with nonstick cooking spray before pouring in your favorite tomato sauces to avoid stains.

What is that stuff on the cake anyway?
When a cake recipe calls for flouring the baking pan, use a bit of the dry cake mix instead and there won't be any white stuff on the outside of the cake.

Hold the Salt
If you accidentally over-salt a dish while it's still cooking, drop in a peeled potato and it will absorb the excess salt.

Sweeter Corn
When boiling corn on the cob, add a pinch of sugar to help bring out the corn's natural sweetness.

Eggsactly
To determine whether an egg is fresh, immerse it in a pan of cool, salted water. If it sinks, it is fresh, but if it rises to the surface, throw it away.

Quick broth – hold the sodium please
For adding chicken flavor without the extra salt and other "stuff" that comes in commercially prepared chicken

broth try the following. The next time you boil chicken or make chicken soup fill empty plastic containers with the juices and freeze. When you need a little chicken flavor, pop one out and toss it into your creation. Two neat holders for small amounts of chicken flavoring are empty yogurt containers and single serving applesauce containers.

Chapter 4
Memory Makers

Self-expression is an excellent way for your child to develop from within. Creating through art, song and play is the work of a child. Need ideas for a craft, song or game? Here are a few for you to choose from. I have broken them down by age groups. First are the craft ideas, next are some games and other activities, then a handful of original songs and finally some recipes for messy and fun mixtures to really get your hands dirty. Enjoy.

Crafts for Infants and Toddlers

Infants and Toddlers can participate in more activities than you think. Infants as young as 6 months, providing they can sit unassisted, can even do art activities. For infants and toddlers I suggest you keep your activities short and sweet since that pretty much describes their attention span. Also, keep them as open ended as possible. What I mean is, don't expect a particular outcome. The most important part of the activity is process not product especially with infants and toddlers. Below I have provided you with art and other activities that have worked well for my children as well as the infants and toddlers I cared for in a school setting.

Art and Crafts for Infants

These three activities are for infants who can sit unassisted.

Shake and Roll
Materials: Clean empty can with a lid, marble, paper, paint and tape

Cut a piece of paper to fit inside the can and insert. Place a little paint at the bottom of the can. Drop a marble in the can and put the lid on. Use tape to secure the lid so that little fingers can't get the lid off. Here comes the fun part. Let your baby shake or roll the can all around. When finished remove the paper to dry. The effect will be a neat splatter pattern.

Table Painting
Materials: Vanilla pudding mix, food color, white paper

Make pudding according to package directions and add food color. Put a blop on the top of the highchair and let them have at it. When they are done, press the white paper on top of the highchair and you have a print of their art. Since this is messy I suggest you strip your baby down to a diaper.

Squeezables
Materials: Two zip lock baggies, two colors of paint

Put two blops of paint, one of each color, into a baggie and seal. Place this baggie into the second baggie and seal. Let your little one squish the two colors together to make a third. They really have fun doing this.

Arts and Crafts for Toddlers

Squish Art
Materials: Zip-Lock bag, shave cream. Red and blue paint and paper

In a zip-lock bag put about a tennis ball size squirt of shaving cream, a squirt of red paint and a squirt of blue paint. Seal the bag! Let your child mix it with their fingers until purple magically appears. Open a small area on one end so they can squeeze the color out onto construction paper and finger paint with it.

Ice Painting
Materials: Ice cube tray, food coloring and paper

Pour water into an ice-cube tray and add food coloring. Put it in the freezer until they are frozen. On a hot day, paint with the colored ice-cubes on the sidewalk or on paper in the sun.

Musical Instruments
Materials: Clean, empty cans with lids, tape, small objects
(rice, beans, buttons, paper clips...) and tape

Fill empty cans or containers with a handful of small
objects. Secure the lids by taping them shut with a strong
tape such as duct tape to discourage those little fingers
from prying the lids off and getting to those little pieces
inside.

Pudding Play
Materials: Vanilla instant pudding mix and food coloring

Make vanilla instant pudding according to package
directions and add food coloring. Drop a tablespoonful on
a paper plate and finger paint! Yummy and fun.

Sponge Painting
Materials: Sponges, scissors, paints and paper or paper
plates
Cut sponges into various shapes and sponge paint on
construction paper or paper plates.

Picture Frames
Materials: Popsicle sticks, glue, markers

Make a picture frame out of popsicle sticks. Decorate
with markers. You can either draw a picture to put in the
frame or find a favorite snapshot to insert.

Necklaces
Materials: Beads, Straws, scissors, yarn, construction
paper, hole punch

Make a necklace by stringing together beads, cut up straws and shapes cut out of construction paper with a hole punched in it.

Paper Horns
Materials: Construction paper, scissors, tape, crayons, stickers

Cut a large circle from construction paper. Decorate the circle with crayons and stickers. Make one cut from the center of the circle to the edge. Curve the paper into a cone shape and tape. Enjoy.

Shake and Roll
Materials: Clean empty can with a lid, marble, paper, paint and tape

Cut a piece of paper to fit inside the can and insert. Place a little paint at the bottom of the can. Drop a marble in the can and put the lid on. Use tape to secure the lid so that little fingers can't get the lid off. Here comes the fun part. Shake or roll the can all around. When finished remove the paper to dry. The effect will be a neat splatter pattern. When dry, paint your child's hand the same color as the paint used in the can and put one print on the paper.

Scribble Art
Materials: Large chunky crayon (easier to grip), various types of drawing medium (paper, cardboard, construction paper, note pad paper, inside of empty cereal boxes etc.)

Using one crayon at a time, let your child color on various types of drawing medium for different effects.

Nature Collage
Materials: Items collected on a nature walk, paper and glue

Go on a nature walk around town. Collect items you see in nature (sticks, leaves, pebbles wild flowers). At home, glue these tiny treasures to a piece of paper.

Arts and Crafts for children 3 years of age and above

The craft ideas that I have included have been amassed from years of teaching in a preschool, creating projects using whatever household items I had on hand with my own children and seeing works done by others and recreating them with my own personal touch. Very few ideas are original and you have probably seen a handful of these ideas in some variation either in a book or hanging on someone's refrigerator. I like to use as many open-ended art activities as possible so that the product is truly original. Read them all and use what you like with your own kids. Personalize as you see fit. But most of all have fun!

Stilts
Materials: Two coffee cans with lids, heavy string, hole punch, duct tape (optional)

Punch two holes about 5 inches apart on both lids. Cut two lengths of string double the length of your child's foot to hip. Thread the string through each can lid ad secure with a not. Be sure the knot is on the underside of the lid. Attach the lids to each can. You can secure each lid even stronger by taping the lids onto the cans with duct tape. To Use: Place each can on the ground and insert your foot between the strings on each can. Hold the string in your hands and walk by pulling gently on the strings as you lift each foot.

Popsicle Stick Puzzles
Materials: 6 Popsicle sticks, markers, paints and brushes, tape

Lay the six Popsicle sticks side by side and tape across the top and bottom. Flip the sticks over and draw a picture with markers or paint on the top of the sticks. When dry peel the tape off the back. Mix them up and try to put them back together to form your picture.

Decorative Pin
Materials: Glue, small puzzle pieces, a jewelry pin, glitter

Collect 3 small puzzle pieces (you can find these at the bottom of any toy box) and layer them one on top of another. Glue them together. When dry, glue them to the backing of a jewelry pin (you can obtain these at any craft store). When completely dry drizzle glue over the puzzle pieces and sprinkle some glitter for added shine.

Popsicle Stick Sun
Materials: 4 popsicle sticks, yellow and orange paint, yellow construction paper, scissors, glue, yellow muffin liner - optional
Paint the Popsicle stick yellow and orange. When dry, glue them together overlapping them on a star fashion to form the rays of the sun. Cut a 2" circle from yellow construction paper and glue to the center of the rays. If you opt for the yellow liner simply glue it to the center of the rays. A nice touch is a happy face in the center.

Paper Plate Flower
Materials: Green construction paper, scissors, glue, small paper dessert plate, paint or markers, glitter (optional) Decorate a small paper dessert plate with markers or paint. Cut out a stem and leaf from the construction paper. When plate is dry glue it to the top of the stem and add the leaf. The plate becomes the flower top. To add sparkle to your flower, dab glue on the paper plate and sprinkle with glitter. Shake off the excess when dry.

A Slice of Summer
Materials: Red and green construction paper, watermelon seeds, scissors, glue

Cut a large green circle and a slightly smaller red circle from construction paper. Glue the red paper circle on top of the green circles. Glue some watermelon seeds on the red circle to make watermelon slices. You can further cut the circles in half or quarters to make halves and wedges.

Paper plate fish
Materials: paper plate, stapler or tape, paint or markers.

Cut a triangle (like a slice of pie, but a bit smaller) out of the plate, and then staple the cut out piece on the opposite end. The missing part becomes the mouth; the cut piece is the tail! Decorate with paint or markers.

Sun Catchers
Materials: Crayon shavings, wax paper, iron, dishtowel, scissors

Cut two same size sheets of wax paper. Lay them on a table. Put crayon shavings on one piece and cover with the second. Lay a dishtowel over the two sheets. With a warm iron press down until the crayon melts and the wax paper sticks together. When cooled, cut your crayon melts into shapes. Hang them in a window.

Bubble Prints
Materials: Paint, bubbles, paper

Add a small amount of paint to your bubble solution. Go outside and blow bubbles in the air. Let your child catch the bubbles on paper. Use different colors. When the bubbles pop, they make a really nice imprint on the paper.

Paper Plate Suns
Materials: Paper plate, scissors, paint, paintbrushes, markers (optional)

Cut triangles around the edge of a paper plate. (This will give it points all around) Paint with yellow and orange paint. If you want to add personality to your sun add facial features with markers when the paint is dry.

Sun Prints
Materials: Construction paper, small objects, glue and glitter

Put three or four small objects on brightly colored paper. Place the papers in a sunny window. After several days, let your child remove the shapes from his paper to reveal the non-faded areas under the shapes. Outline the non-faded areas with glue and sprinkle on glitter.

Bubble Art
Materials: Bubbles, straw, cup, food coloring, white paper

In a cup mix bubble solution with food coloring. Put a straw into the cup of bubble mixture and blow until bubbles are on top of the cup. DO NOT DRINK the bubble solution. Lay a piece of paper on top of the bubbles and the design will show up on the paper.

Butterfly Feet
Materials: White paper, pipe cleaners, feet, colored construction paper

Have your child stand with his feet together on a piece of white construction paper. Trace around the shoes to create a butterfly outline. Give your child a precut piece of construction paper for the body to be placed in the middle of the butterfly. Let your child decorate his butterfly as he or she wishes. Add pipe cleaners for the antennae.

Coffee Filter Butterflies
Materials: Two coffee filters, pipe cleaner, food color, eyedropper

Flatten two coffee filter and pinch them together add secure them with a pipe cleaner. Using an eyedropper drop highly concentrated food coloring onto the butterflies. This creates wonderful designs and blends of colors. Allow them to sit aside of awhile to dry.

Bug Catchers
Materials: Oatmeal containers with a lid, glue or tape, screen or netting, yarn.

Cut a large window in the side and glue or tape screen or netting to inside of the window. Decorate the bug catchers with paint. Put the lid on top and punch holes at the top to put in yarn for the handle.
*Remember to let your bugs go free at the end of the day.

Feet Butterflies
Materials: Paint, paper, feet, markers, pan or tray

Dip bare feet in a pan with paint. Step onto a piece of paper with heels together and the feet pointing outward. When dry add antennas with marker.

Ladybug Prints
Materials: Red ink pads or red paint, white paper, black markers.

Press your child's thumb on red stamp pads or in red paint and make thumbprints on pieces of white paper. Then turn the thumbprints into ladybugs by adding dots and six legs to each print they made.

Paper Plate Ladybugs
Materials: Two paper plates, black and red paint, paintbrush, scissors, glue, black pipe cleaners and a brad

Paint the bottom of one paper plate black and paint the other red. Cut the red plate in half. Attach the red halves to the black plate about 2" from the top. Dip your finger in the black paint and add Ladybug spots to the red backs. Glue pipe cleaners at the top for antennae.

Spiders
Materials: Egg carton, black paint, pipe cleaners, wiggle eyes, glue

Use 1 section of an egg carton and, paint black, add pipe cleaners for legs and wiggle eyes.

Grow Your Own Garden
Use an egg carton to grow your own garden. Fill each section of the carton with potting soil. Have your child use a finger to poke a hole in the center of each section. After placing a bean seed (soak beans overnight) or a few

marigold seeds in each hole, make sure to cover the seeds gently with soil. Water each section of the carton making sure not to over water. Place the garden in a sunny windowsill, water as needed, and enjoy watching your garden grow.

Dry Leaves
Materials: Green construction paper, dry fall leaves picked up from the ground, glue, brushes
Cut a fairly large leaf shape from construction paper for each child. Have the children brush glue on their leaf shapes. Then let them crinkle dry leaves and scatter the pieces all over the glue.

Leaf People
Materials: Leaves, glue, paper, crayons
Glue leaves to a piece of construction paper. The leaves are the bodies. With crayons add a head, arms and legs.

Paper Plate Apples
Materials: Paper plate, green construction paper, apple seeds
Paint the backs of paper plates red to make 'apple halves.' When the paint has dried, attach precut construction paper leaves and stems. Then glue a few apple seeds in the centers of the white sides of their plates

Leaf Rubbings
Materials, Leaves, paper, crayons

To help your child notice the veins in leaves and the different shapes of leaves, Place a variety of leaves (underside up) under a piece of light colored construction paper. Using the sides of crayons that have had the paper covering removed, gently rub the crayon over the leaves to make an imprint of the leaves.

Fall wreath
Materials: toilet paper rolls, paint (brown, red, yellow, orange), paintbrush, tissue paper (brown, yellow, red, orange), string and glue.

Paint the toilet paper rolls with fall colors and/or glue on fall colored pieces of tissue paper. When dry string them together for a nice fall wreath to hang on your door or wall.

Fall Tree
Materials: Paper plate, brown paper, fall colored tissue paper, scissors and glue.
Cut a trunk out of the brown paper and attach to the paper plate (full side out). Tear the tissue paper into small pieces and glue to the plate for fall leaves.

Snow Gauge
Materials a large empty coffee can, ruler, marking pen (permanent ink).
Place the ruler inside the can. Mark and number inches onto the inside of the can.
When it snows, place the can outside in a clear place.
When it stops snowing, you and your children can tell how deep the snow is by noting which inch mark it has reached.

Snow Scene
Materials: Blue construction paper, packaging chips, glue

Give your child a sheet of pale blue construction paper and Styrofoam packaging chips. Let them create a winter scene. These turn out to be lovely three-dimensional projects.

Snowflakes
Materials: Honeycomb cereal, white paint, glue, and blue construction paper.

Paint honeycomb cereal white. When dry glue them to blue construction paper for a snowy scene.

Winter Flowers
Materials: Egg cartons, light blue pipe cleaners, light blue construction paper, glue, light blue paint, glitter and scissors.
Cut the sections of an egg carton apart. Paint each of them light blue, both inside and out. When dry poke a hole through the center and insert a pipe cleaner. Knot the pipe cleaner so it does not go back through the hole. Using a paintbrush, brush glue over the flower and sprinkle with glitter. Cut a leaf shape out of light blue construction paper. Poke a hole in the leaf and insert he pipe cleaner through it. When dry put them in a vase.

Mittens
Materials needed: Colored construction paper, crayons, scissors, markers and string

Cut out mitten two shapes from colored construction paper and decorate with crayons or markers. Attach a string to the bottom of each and hang.

Newspaper Snowmen
Materials needed: Newspaper, scissors, stapler, paint, scraps of material
Trace 2 large snowmen from newspaper sections and cut out. Paint them white. When dry staple the two together,

painted side out leaving an opening at the bottom. Stuff with crumbled pieces of newspaper. When finished staple the bottom. Finish decorating eyes, buttons, scarf etc...

Music Shakers
Materials: Toilet paper or paper towel tubes, paper, crayons, tape, rice or beans, wax paper, rubber bands

Wrap some toilet paper or paper towel tubes with paper colored with crayons. Cover one end with wax paper held in place with rubber bands and fill with some rice or beans and then cover the other end with wax paper secured with rubber bands. Shake to music.

Tambourines
Materials: 2 paper plates, crayons, paints, stickers, glue or stapler, streamers

Decorate the backs of two paper plates with crayons, paints, pieces of colored paper etc. Put some rice on one plate and glue or staple the second plate to the first with the decorated sides out. You can glue some streamers to the outside edges for an added look.

Necklaces
Materials: Ziti shells, paint, string

Paint ziti shells with paint. When dry string them together to make a necklace.

Bird Feeder
Materials: Pinecone, peanut butter, bird seed, string

Spread some peanut butter on a pinecone and then roll it in birdseed. Attach a string to the pinecone and hang outside.

Games for Infants

Here are two tried and true games for your little ones.

Peek-A-BOO!
How to play:
Sit in front of your baby and get his attention. When he looks at you, cover your face with your hands and say "Peek-A-Boo!" Then uncover your face and smile. Repeat. You can use a blanket to cover your face instead of your hands. Stop this game at once if it is frightening to your child.

Where is /Name/'s _____?
How to play:
Sit facing your baby and get her attention by calling her name or stroking her cheek with your finger. Say, "Where is Angela's nose?" Then touch the body part you named and say, "There's your _____! Repeat changing the body part. Discontinue if your child shows boredom or appears to be upset.

Games for Toddlers

*Star Ball
How to play:
This is similar to the game, Hot Potato. Children sit on the ground with their legs apart and toes touching someone else's. This makes a sort of star or sun pattern on the ground. Each child takes turns rolling the ball to another within the boundaries of the legs while music is played. The person to whom the ball is rolled is to gently push the ball to another player. When the music stops the person

with the ball is removed from the game. Continue until there is one person left.

*Popcorn Ball
How to play:
Each child is to hold a portion of a sheet until it is taut. Put one or more balls in the middle of the sheet. Begin shaking the sheet up and down and try to keep the balls, "Popcorn", in the popper.

*Red Light, Green Light
How to play:
One child plays the "Traffic Guard" and the rest try to touch him/her. At the start, all the children form a line about 15 feet away from the traffic guard. The Traffic Guard faces away from the line of kids and says "green light". Only at this time are the rest of the kids allowed to move towards the Traffic Guard. At any point, the Traffic Guard may say "red light!" and turn around. If any of the kids are caught moving after this has been said, they must go back to the starting line. Play resumes when the Traffic Guard turns back around and says "green light". The Traffic Guard wins if all the kids are out before anyone is able to touch him/her. Otherwise, the first player to touch the Traffic Guard wins the game and earns the right to be "Traffic Guard" for the next game.

*Hide –N-Seek
How to play:
One child is "it" and covers his eyes and begins to count to 25. While "it" is counting the other children scatter and hide. When "it" has reached the number 25 he is to yell, "ready or not here I come". At this point he is allowed to open his eyes and start searching for the rest of the players. When you are found you are to sit where "it" did the counting. You win if "it" is unable to find you. If you

are the winner you can be "it" next. If there is no winner, then "it" chooses the next person to be "it".

Variation for toddlers: You hide a toy or stuffed animal while you help your child count to 10. You can both look for the hidden stuffed animal.

*Pillow Hopping
How to play:
Spread some pillows on the floor in a large open area. Begin hopping from one to the other. Pretend the floor is water and the pillows are either rocks or icebergs. The object is not to fall into the "water". If you fall in you are out.

*Wiggle Wiggle Freeze
How to play:
The children are to stand facing you. You are to stand with your back to the children. When you say, "Wiggle" they are to wiggle and jiggle all about until you say, "Freeze". When the children hear the word freeze they are to stop moving and hold their position. You are to immediately turn around after saying "freeze" and try to catch someone moving. If you do they are out.

*Bubble Poppers
How to play:
On a nice day go out and blow some bubbles. The children are to run around the yard and try to pop as many bubbles as they can before they reach the ground. Bubbles that have reached the ground can be stepped on but the object is to get them before they hit grass.

Games for Ages 3 and above

In addition to the following games, those described in the Toddler Games section denoted with an asterik* also work well with this age group.

Games from the Toddler Games section include: Star Ball, Popcorn Ball, Red Light Green Light, Hide-N- Seek, Pillow Hopping, Wiggle Wiggle Freeze and Bubble Poppers

Duck, Duck, Goose
How to Play:
In this game, children sit down in a circle facing each other. One person is "it" and walks around the circle. As they walk around, they gently tap each child's head and call out
"Duck" or "Goose". If they are called "Duck" they do nothing but if they are called "Goose" they get up and try to chase "it" around the circle. The goal is to tap that person before they are able sit down in the "Goose's" spot. If the "Goose" is not able to do this, they become "it" for the next round and play continues. If they do tap the "it" person, the person tagged has to sit in the center of the circle called "The Goose Pot". Then the "Goose" becomes it for the next round. The person in the Goose Pot is not allowed to come out until another person is tagged and they are replaced.

Mother May I?
How to Play:
One person stands facing away from a line of kids and is called "Mother". She then chooses a child either at random, or in order and tells that child that he/she may take' x number of ' giant/regular/baby steps either forward or backward. The child responds with "Mother may I?" The "Mother" then states, "Yes" or "No", depending on her whim, and the child complies. If the child forgets to

ask, "Mother may I?" he/she goes back to the starting line. The first one to touch Mother wins.

Variation: Each child takes turns asking, "Mother may I take 'x number' steps?" And the child who is mother replies yes or no. In addition to baby, regular, and giant steps, you can make up any type of silly steps for example "Frankenstein steps or ballerina steps.

I Spy
How to play:
One person says, " I spy with my little eye, something that is.... (Color, shape or size)". The others try to guess what the object is and the one who guesses it takes the next turn.

Follow the Leader
How to play:
One person is chosen to be "The Leader". The rest of the children are to imitate "The Leader" in whatever they do or wherever they go. "The Leader" can choose the next leader after his/her specified time is up.

Simon Says
How to play:
Children form a line facing "The Leader", who performs any action preceded by the words "Simon says do this". If he doesn't say, "Simon says" before an action then anyone who imitates the action is out of the game. Continue until one person is left.

Over and Under

How to play:

Children are to stand in a line with their feet wide apart. The child in front will hand a ball over their head to the child behind who must pass the ball between his legs to the child behind him. This continues over the head and under their bodies until it gets to the last child. This child is to go to the front of the line and continue the over and under game. The game is over when everyone has had a turn being first in line.

Tickle Tag
How to play:
One person is "It". The rest of the children scatter as "It" tries to tag them. Tickling the players as they get caught gets them out of the game. The first person to be tickled is the next "It".

Statue
How to play:
One child is the "sculptor" who creates statues. The other children are lumps of clay waiting to be molded. The "Sculptor" goes to each child in turn and moves its body parts into position to create a statue. The statue is to stay in the same position until all of the other lumps of clay have been molded. The first statue to move is the next sculptor.

More Fun Activities To Do with Infants

Cuddle them often and respond lovingly to their cries. This may be difficult if they are colic but do your best to sooth them and meet their needs. By doing this you will not only gain a special bond with your child but your child will come to learn they can count on you to be there for them.

Give them opportunities to practice new physical abilities. When they can hold their head steady try pulling them up to a sitting position. Later on try pulling them to a standing position. Let them bounce on their feet. Give them "belly time" so they can strengthen their neck muscles and practice rolling over.

Provide them opportunities to listen to language and imitate sounds. Talk about what you are doing whether it is changing a diaper, giving them a bath or folding clothes name as many objects and body parts as possible. Sing songs to them, if you don't know any make them up. They don't have to make sense because babies are not music critics they just love to hear your voice.

Provide them with safe objects to look at, pat, roll, touch, taste and examine. Let them feel as many textures as possible. Talk to them about the feel, color or sound and object makes. When they can sit up give them pots and spoons to bang. Remember, the best toy of all is you.

Since their attention spans are extremely short, play only while your baby is interested and happy. Watch for signs that your baby has had enough and then move on. Some signs include looking away or bored, pushing objects away that just moments earlier brought a smile to their faces and of course crying which in itself can mean many things.

Read stories together

Go for a walk outdoors and point out as many things as you can.

If weather permits sit in the grass in bare feet

Fill up a small container of water and let your baby splash
– Never leave baby unattended near water

More Fun Activities To Do with Toddlers

Drape a sheet or large blanket over some chairs and
pretend you are camping out or that you are a bear in a
cave.

Get out some hair clips, combs and brushes and play
Barber/Beauty shop

On a clean table spray some shaving cream and swish it
around with your hands. Use pacifier with little ones if
they try to put it in their mouths.

If the season it right and the weather is nice go out and
find as many colored leaves as you can and glue them on
a piece of paper as a Fall collage.

Make a game out of clean up. See how many red things
you can put away, See how many soft things you can put
away…

Do some silly dancing to music

Read a book together.

Find some old clothes and play dress up

If the weather is nice, run through a sprinkler.

If you have enough snow on the ground make a snowman or two.

Make snow angels if the weather permits.

Rake some leaves into a pile and jump in – repeat.

Pretend to be sailors or go fishing in your living room. A couch makes a nice boat.

Line up your kitchen chairs and pretend to be a train by crawling through the tunnel it makes.

Plant a small garden or a flower in clean yogurt containers.

If weather will permit, lie on your back outside and see what kinds of shapes you can find in the clouds.

See how many different animal sounds you can make.

See how many things you can do standing in one place. For example: jump up and down, spin around, roll your shoulders, stretch your arms, roll your head from side to side, make each other giggle, make a silly face, hop on one foot, clap your hands

Bang on pots and pans with a wooden spoon.

Have a picnic in the great outdoors. If the weather is bad outside have a picnic inside.

Blow some bubbles.

Toss small objects into a bucket or laundry basket.

Make faces in a large mirror together.

Stack food boxes or cans on top of another (count how many you can stack before they fall over).

Sort socks by color

Sing, "Old McDonald Had a Farm" and not only make the sound of the animals but act them out!

Brush each other's teeth.

If it is raining pretend to be a duck. Put on your rubber boots and raincoat and go puddle jumping.

Make home made cookies together. (Great math experience by counting and measuring your ingredients.)

Use a piece of yarn and make shapes on the floor with it. Have your child guess the shape.

Stack things

Sort things by size, color or shape

Toss a ball into a laundry basket

Read stories every day

Turn the lights down, get a comfy pillow and blanket, lie on the floor and take a nap.

More Fun Activities for Ages 3 and Above

Paint with things other than paintbrushes. Some ideas are cotton balls, noses, toes, fingers, pinecones, pine tree branches, leaves, feathers, sponges, wheels of a toy car, and string. Don't be limited to these use anything!
*Hint - For easy clean up add dish soap to the paints.

Chalk drawings on paper of many varieties are fun. To eliminate the dust dip them in water before you color.

Draw a letter or number on your partners back with your finger. Your partner is to guess the number or letter.

Stretch rubber bands over open shoeboxes, canisters etc. and listen to the sound they make when plucked.

Act out your favorite story.

Make a telephone out of two paper cups or foam cups and string. Talk all you want this is a free call.

Gather some sticks, small rocks, leaves, grass or indoor items such as a piece of clothing, a piece of fruit, a sponge... Use a magnifying glass to see what interesting things you can find close up!

Take an old T- Shirt and decorate it using markers made for clothing.
Make a "Fun Things" box. Fill a fairly nice sized box with things that you think would be fun to have on a rainy day. Some things to be included: paper, crayons, string,

old greeting cards, glue, paint, buttons, unmatched socks, lunch bags, felt, empty toilet paper or paper towel rolls, scissors, paper cups, hole punch, puzzle pieces (from a puzzle that is missing pieces) board games, cards, magazines.... Be creative! Decorate the outside of this box with markers, paint.... And label it "MY FUN BOX"

Go for a walk and count the number of things you can find for one or more of the following categories: shape, color, size, texture...

Try to walk from one room to another balancing an object on your head.

Fill a bag with household items and try to guess what they are by sticking your hand in the bag and feeling the object. Be careful not to put anything with a sharp point in the bag.

If the weather is nice go out and play silly relay games. Try to run backwards, sideways, crawling on your hands and knees, rolling on the ground...

Tell a story about your worst day and your best day.

Play Guess What I See. You choose an abject and try to describe it without saying what it is. Your partner will try to guess the object. You can respond to the guesses can be "yes" or "no" or "warm" or "cold".

Look through magazines and try to find pictures of things that begin with a certain letter of the alphabet. You can even cut them out and glue them on paper and make a book.

Look through magazines and try to find pictures of groups of things for a certain number. For example: Look for two of something; it could be two children, two dogs, two people, and two apples…. You can cut them out and make a number book.

Decorate some paper towel rolls with crayons or paint and use as a telescope.

Play Pin the Nose on the Snowman

Mitten Hunt – get as many pairs of gloves as you can find. Hide one from each set around the house. Put the other mitten in a bag. Each child pulls a mitten from the bag. Their mission is to find the other matching mitten.

Winter fun - Pour water into different size plastic containers and add food coloring. Freeze. When ready to play, loosen the frozen blocks by letting them slightly defrost then take them out and make colorful snow/ice creations.

Songs

Children of all ages love to sing and dance. Singing or humming a catchy tune can put a smile on your face and even make tedious tasks fun. The following songs are my very own original lyrics put to familiar children's tunes. Have fun with them. You can even create your own. Simply pick a tune and sing about events you are doing or things you are observing. It doesn't have to make much sense as long as you are having fun. Sometimes the sillier the words the better the song.

Getting Clean

As you are getting clean either at the tub or sink the following little tunes with help get the job done. Sing the appropriate verse as you clean each body part. Don't forget to wash behind your ears!

"In the Tub" (Tune: This is the way the Ladies ride)
This is the way I wash my hair, wash my hair, wash my hair
This is the way I wash my hair, when I'm in the tub
Additional verses: This is the way I wash my: face, hands, belly legs, feet, ears etc…

"Peeps and Dirty Cheeks" (Tune: Camptown Races")
You've got peeps and dirty cheeks, doo daa doo daa
You've got peeps and dirty cheeks, Oh, the doo daa day
You're gonna peep all night, You're gonna peep all day
You've got peeps and dirty cheeks, Oh, the doo daa day

"Brush Your Teeth" (Tune: Row, Row, Row Your Boat)

I brush, brush, brush my teeth
I brush them just like so
Back and forth and up and down
Away the cavities go

Cleaning up the house

Who else besides children need a boost for picking up their toys? Here is a song to sing while the work gets done.

"I'm Picking Up My Toys" (Tune: Won't You Be My Darlin')
I'm picking up my toys and I'm putting them away
I'm picking up my toys and I'm putting them away
I'm picking up my toys and I'm putting them away, right where they belong

Winter

When the holidays are over and you are tired of singing "Jingle Bells" and "Rudolph" here is a few songs to celebrate snow.

"Nine Little Snowflakes" (Tune: 1 Little 2 Little 3 Little Indians)
As you sing this song hold up the appropriate number of fingers. When you get to the last verse wiggle your fingers down to the ground.

1 little, 2 little, 3 little snowflakes
4 little, 5 little, 6 little snowflakes
7 little, 8 little, 9 little snowflakes

Falling on the ground

"I'm a Happy Snowfriend" (Tune: I'm a Little Teapot)
I'm a happy snowfriend
White and fat
Here is my broomstick
Here is my hat
When the warm sun shines down on me
I melt and melt away you see

"Snowflakes" (Tune: If You're Happy and You Know It)
There are snowflakes in my hair, in my hair
There are snowflakes in my hair, in my hair
There are snowflakes in my hair and I don't even care
There are snowflakes in my hair, in my hair
There are snowflakes on my nose, on my nose
There are snowflakes on my nose, on my nose
There are snowflakes on my nose and some fell on my toes
There are snowflakes on my nose, on my nose

Spring
As the snow begins to melt away we look forward to warmer weather, new flowers and of course rain. Yes we look forward to rain, how else would we get all of those fun puddles to jump in?

"Rain" (Tune: Row, Row, Row Your Boat)
Rain, rain falling down
Falling on the ground
Make a puddle just for me
So I can slash around

"A Happy Garden" (Tune: The Farmer in the Dell)
First we plant the seeds
First we plant the seeds
Hi Ho and so we grow
First we plant the seeds
The sun begins to shine (2x's)
Hi Ho and so we grow
The sun begins to shine
The rain begins to fall (2x's)
Hi Ho and so we grow
The rain begins to fall
The plants begin to grow (2 x's)
Hi Ho and so we grow
The plants begin to grow
The flowers smile at us (2x's)
Hi Ho and so we grow
The Flowers smile at us

Summer

We all look forward to summer. The sun, bathing suits, picnics, but mostly the sun. Here are two songs to get you happy in the summer time.

"I'm a Little Fishy" (Tune: I'm a Little Teapot)
I'm a little fishy that loves to swim
Here is my tail, here is my fin
When I want to have fun with my friends
I call to them – Jump right in!

"My Sunshine" (Tune: You are my Sunshine)

You are my sunshine, my yellow sunshine
You are warm on summer days
I like to play when you are shinning down on me
Please come out and take the gray days away

Fall

As the days turn cooler we watch as the trees turn colors and the leaves fall. What could be better than to jump right into a great big pile of red, yellow and orange leaves? I couldn't come up with anything either. Enjoy my tribute to fall leaves.

"Nine Little Leaves" (Tune: 1 Little, 2 Little, 3 Little Leaves)
1 little, 2 little, 3 little yellow leaves
4 little, 5 little, 6 little red leaves
7 little, 8 little, 9 little orange leaves
Falling from the trees

"Leaves" (Tune: If Your Happy and You Know It)
Leaves are falling on the ground, on the ground
Leaves are falling on the ground, on the ground
Yellow, orange, red and brown
Leaves are falling on the ground
Leaves are falling on the ground on the ground

About Me

Here are a few songs about various body parts. Point to them as you sing.

"Parts of Me" (Tune: If You're Happy and You Know It)
My ears help me hear sounds both soft and loud
My eyes let me see blue skies and white clouds
Oh my nose is there tell me if a dirty diaper's near
And my mouth can taste a cookie and give a cheer!

"I have two Hands" (Tune: Twinkle, Twinkle Little Star)
I have two hands that reach up high
I can almost touch the sky
Slowly, slowly down they go
I can even touch my toes
I have two hands now don't you see
They're for hugging you and me

"My Hands" This was never put to a tune but you can sing song it.
My hands can clap
My feet can tap
My body spins round and round
I can jump way up high
And I can touch the ground

Messy Mixtures

The following recipes are as fun to do as the product they create. Enjoy them. There are many different recipes out there but these have worked well for me over the years.

Big Crayons
Crayons (pieces or whole)
Foil cupcake liners

Chop crayons into small pieces. Line baking sheets with foil liners and fill to the top with crayon bits. Heat your oven to 250 degrees and cook until melted. Let them cool completely and peel away the foil.

Bubble Solution
1 c water
2 tbl Light Karo Syrup OR 2 tbl glycerine
4 tbl dishwashing liquid (Green Dawn and Clear Ivory work well)

Mix above ingredients together. Use any type of bubble blowing wand and enjoy!

Flour and Salt Clay
4 c flour   1 c salt
Food coloring
water to moisten

Mix above ingredients to desired dampness. Store in refrigerator to avoid spoiling. This clay dries hard and can be painted. For re-useable clay, add 2 tbl cooking oil to the mixture.

Playdough
1c flour	½ c salt
1 tbl oil	1 tsp cream of tartar
1 c water	food coloring

Put all ingredients in a saucepan, cook over medium heat until dough pulls away from the sides of pan and forms a ball. Remove from heat and cool. Knead until smooth. Store in an airtight container.

Pudding Paint
Instant vanilla pudding
Food coloring

Mix pudding according to package directions. Add food coloring. Paint on paper plates. This is not only art it is edible, Mmmmm! (Great for young artists who can't seem to keep their hands out of their mouths.)

Texture Paint
Food Coloring Flour
Salt   Water

Mix equal amounts of flour salt and water together. Add food coloring to achieve your desired color. Children enjoy various textures for finger painting. It also adds a dimensional effect to their artwork.

Finger Paint
½ c Flour   ½ c Water
1 tbsp liquid detergent
Food Coloring

Mix the above ingredients together and pint on paper, cardboard etc.

Chapter 5
Something For Parents

There will be days when you feel as if you are the only parent who is staying home with their children. When you find yourself looking forward to discussing the use of the 9-digit zip codes over 5-digit zip codes with your mailman it is time to get out. Because of little odds and ends you try to accomplish during the day or snags set off by tantrum throwing children you may not make it out to socialize with other parents and children as much as you would like. Maybe you don't know of any other stay at home parents in your area. Whichever the case may be there are ways you can get out and meet others who do what you do. Not only will it benefit your children by having friends of similar ages to interact with but you too will gain friends who share your situation. These newfound friends understand your grief and are a wonderful outlet for venting. Since they are also home with their children dealing with tantrums, boredom, sillies and so forth they may be able to share with you tricks of their own to combat some of your problem spots and vice versa.

Isolation Busters

Where to find other at home parents

Don't know where to find these comrades? Here are a few places to check out

1. Libraries, they often have story hour for different age groups. Call ahead to find out the times and attend a few readings. You are bound to find a friend or two there.

2. Local playgrounds are also a nice place to meet stay at home parents. Go often and at different times of the day. If you don't meet anyone at least the fresh air with do you and your children a world of good.

3. There are local organizations for Stay at home Parents. These groups usually meet once a month at a public place, libraries, church basements, youth halls etc. These are wonderful organizations to join. The cost is very minimal (sometimes free) and usually covers an entire year. Newsletters are sent out with a calendar of play dates and events for the month. Playgroups are also available, if you choose, within the organization. Parents and their children can join different committees within the club depending on hobbies and special interests. Most clubs also do some charitable work for the community. If these clubs are not advertising in your local paper call your local library, church and youth centers to see if regular meetings are held by any of these groups.

4. Check the yellow pages in your phone book for music groups or tumbling classes. These cost more

but hey, it's another option and the kids tend to like it.

5. Lastly go on-line and search for stay at home parents. There are many great sites and chats for parents who stay at home. Some are very informative and some are just plain fun.

Keep in touch with the outside world by listening to the news at least for 20 minutes each day. To do this simply turn off the children's television program, they could use a break from it anyway, and tune into the radio before the happy songs tape goes in. That way you will not be shocked to learn about world events and changes from previewing your child's history homework.

Stress Reducers

So you think that all of your days are going to be mud pies and kisses? Well they won't be and the sooner you accept this the better off you will be. While there is no magical wand-waving spell that can make a bad day terrific there are a few things you can do to make the day better. In my experiences both as a mom and as an Early Childhood Educator of young children I have found a few "tricks" that can turn some frowns right side up thus lowering your level of stress. Allow me to tell you what makes my days stressful and how I change it.

I find that my most stressful days occur when I am paying too much attention to housework i.e. cleaning, laundry, dishes, the computer or the phone and not enough attention to my kids. They see that I am preoccupied and they miss me even though I am in the same room with them. These are the times when they get crazy and act out. Their voice level peaks at about 10 and they begin to do things they know they shouldn't. To eliminate this I simply stop doing whatever it is I am doing and call out "Story Time". We sit down together and read a book. Just by doing this I get them to sit, get quiet and relax. After one or two stories I can sometimes enlist a little help with the housework but I don't always count on it. Between dusting and doing dishes I play a quick game of hide and seek. Bear in mind that kids want to be a part of your activities too. Remember, the housework will always wait. I also try not to make "bad" choices. For instance, if the kids are starting to act out I don't pack them up to run errands. If you do this you will certainly increase your stress level and make their meltdown happen at an alarming rate. If you find you or the children need to blow off steam do something silly together. Remember if you laugh you can't get mad.

15 Stress Reducers to do with your children

1. Use the recipe in the Messy Mixtures section of this book for washable finger paint and paint each other's faces.

2. Take a pillowcase and stuff it with dirty laundry. Tie the end with a string and kick it around the living room. This is a great stress reliever and no one gets hurt.

3. Plant jellybeans in your garden. I know nothing will grow but it's fun to talk about what might happen if something did grow. What would it look

like? What would it taste like? What color would it be? How tall would it be? How would we cook it? See, language skills are developing here.

4.   Bake some cupcakes and have a birthday party for one or more stuffed animal friends.

5.   Tickle each other.

6.   Break out the play-dough and have at it. This activity relieves a lot of stress. Think about it, you can pound away all of your troubles and create the flattest blue pancake ever.

7.   Water works wonders; try splashing in a big pail of it. If it's raining outside or just too cold then fill the tub and splash away.

8.   Bake cookies together. Yum!

9.   Pull out some old clothes (which you should have in a box for play anyway) and put on a play. Make up the story as you go along.

10.   Sing silly versus to well loved songs.

11.   Put socks on your hands and mittens on your feet and try to walk on your hands

12.   Have a pillow fight. Remember no hitting in the face!

13.   Tie one of your legs together with one of your child's and attempt to walk around the house. This takes practice and teamwork.

14. Play Wiggle, Wiggle Stop! You turn with your back to the kids and say wiggle, wiggle, wiggle--- STOP! The children move about when you say wiggle and they are to freeze when you say stop. You then turn around and try to catch someone moving. If you do you are to tickle them until they say, "stop".

15. Sprinkle pillows on the floor and do some pillow hopping. You can pretend to be frogs hopping on lily pads – try not to fall in the "water".

"I am now a g'ma- this is one of my favorites when young moms are at their wit's end! Put kid, kids in tub, in very little water. Let the water trickle. Blow bubbles or give them lots of water toys, or cups, spoons etc to play with. While they play, sit on the bathroom floor and read a magazine. This is a great stress reliever for all, and kids are much happier after a long water playtime. You can cook a meal while child stands on a sturdy chair at the sink and plays. Just trickle the water, if sink begins to fill, empty."

Kathy S., Mommy of 3 grown children,
Grandma of 1 special grandson.

Myths and Realities of Stay-At-Home Parents

There are a few myths that surround Stay-At-Home Parents that I would like to address. You will inevitably hear people convey these myths to you in one form or another. It may be a casual comment or a flat out sarcastic remark. In whatever fashion you hear it just smile at their ignorance and go on enjoying your life and your children. They obviously never stayed home to raise children and if they did and still make such remarks – they either had lots of help or they simply don't recall what it was like.

I can remember commenting to an office-working friend of mine about having so much to do around the holidays. Her reply to me was "If I didn't have to work and was home all day I would have been finished with my holiday stuff weeks ago". My reply was simply "Me Too." She looked puzzled and I didn't offer any further explanation I decided to let her figure it out. Don't fall into the trap of thinking that you should be able to do it all since you do not leave the house each morning and go to an office. Believe me as a stay at home parent you work just as hard if not harder than most people.

Following the myths are reality checks to either confirm your thoughts or enlighten you on what really happens.

Myth #1
Since we are home all day we have plenty of time each day to clean the house spotlessly and have all laundry items clean, pressed and put away.

Myth #2

Since we are home all day we should be organized and have no problem paying the bills on time not to mention having holiday gifts bought and wrapped by December 1.

Myth #3
Since we are home all day we have plenty of time to make 3 course meals served on time and with a smile.

Myth #4
Since we are home all day we should have no problem running errands all over town i.e. the post office, dry cleaners, grocery store etc...

The only truth or fraction of truth I can find in any of these myths is that we are home all day. I can't even say that we are in the home all day. If you were blessed with a nature-loving child like my son you will begin your day at 6:00 with breakfast followed by relentless requests to go outside. If it was not raining by 7am the request had turned into a frenzy of clothing and body parts as he tried to get dressed as fast as a 1 yr old could in order to get out of the house. Yes, I used to wave to neighbors while in my yard with my son as they drove off to work at the ungodly hour of 7:30am. They probably thought I was nuts to be out when the dew hadn't even dried on the grass. If the weather was exceptionally good diaper changes, snack, lunch, and sometimes naps were conducted outside. So to say we are home all day to complete the tasks we are theoretically supposed to complete depends on whether you are in the house or out.

So what myth should I tackle first? Will it be the cooking, cleaning, laundry, paying bills or taking care of errands? Let me begin by clearing up what the myths have left out – We may be "home" all day but so are the kids!

Myth Reality Check

Myth #1 - Cleaning.

Children have a knack for undoing most anything faster than you can blink. You say you got around to cleaning the house today? Think again, toys will be sprinkled around as soon as you pick them up off the floor, drawings and crayons cover the table you just finished cleaning, that basket of laundry you and your children helped you to fold has "fallen" over because the Indianapolis 500 was taking place in your house and your children neglected to tell you the basket was on the track. You sometimes feel as if you clean the same room (kitchen, family room, dining room – take your pick) over and over all day long. You are! What's next? Laundry? Ok. Let's say you are able to get one load into the washer and between the diapers, snacks, meals, straitening up, play, disarming battles and kissing ouches you may actually get that load into the dryer with another in the washer but that is where it usually ends. In order to remove the dryer load it must get into a basket and folded. The basket part is no problem hence the washer load makes it into the dryer. Then the problem becomes reality. Until you fold and put away the first load the dryer load might as well get use to its new home for a day or two. You may even bypass the dresser stage and use the clothing straight from the basket. The load in the dryer may never make it to the basket stage and simply get used strait from its new metal and enamel home.

Myth #2 - Paying the Bills

Ok, what could be so difficult about opening your checkbook, writing out a check and slipping it into an envelope? Children. They seem to be fascinated by paperwork, pens and stamps. Just try to keep stamps away from a child who has just leaned about stickers. Envelopes are another intriguing item. Paper that is a pocket – how fun. I wonder what a 2 or 3 year old can put inside one of these? How about a cookie? Usually the cookie is soggy from pre-tasting. I dare you to write the correct check amount or the correct payee while your inquisitive 3 year old is bombarding you with questions. Paying bills – good luck! I'm not even going to touch holiday shopping or wrapping – I will let you're your imagination take this one on.

Myth #3 - Cooking

Will there be dinner? Usually, will it be a three-course meal with fresh ground pepper on the salad? No. If your children take naps you might be able to prepare a nutritious meal but salad, main course and dessert – Ha! Those little helpers will try their best in the kitchen to lend a hand and you may surprise yourself and your husband once in a while but be happy if the meal is cooked and the kids eat it.

Myth #4 – Errands Around Town

Last but not least taking care of those around the town errands. I love this one. I challenge you to stop into the grocery store or quick stop shop for milk and bread and make it out in minutes. You may get the milk and bread and get into line ok but what about the candy rack right where you are waiting? I swear they put these there just to torment parents. And who else can make a quick stop into the post office a nightmare? Children. In a matter of minutes your sweet usually well-mannered children can pull out and sprinkle around the post office piles of certified receipts that are conveniently placed in open-ended slots on the side of service desks. While you frantically try to pick them up they have invaded the P.O. Box area and are going from box to box spinning the little combination levers. Display racks with stickers and padded envelopes are also fun for little ones. Watch your children; hold on to their hands you may say. Do you know the speed and agility of a child who sees tempting things and has an uncontrollable desire to "touch" them? Not every trip to every outside vendor is lunacy but count on it being more than just a quick run in.

Can you ever get anything accomplished? Yes. Will it be everything on your "To Do List" everyday? No. Some days are better for accomplishing "grown-up" tasks than others. Assess each day and proceed accordingly.

Words of Wisdom

Every day brings about different challenges for both children and parents alike. Find the fun each challenge holds and you will make life that much more enjoyable. Your children are young once, enjoy everything they have to share with you and share with them the most precious thing you have to give – yourself!

So include your children in as much as possible, kiss and hug them often and praise them repeatedly.

"This too shall pass and be a memory." It applies equally to the good and the bad parts of parenthood. There will

be an end to the diapers and to the sleepless nights. But there will also be an end to the warmth of a baby snuggling up to you, so treasure those moments and store up happy memories."

Eleanor W., Mommy of Two and Grandma of Two, Washington

"Don't compare your kid to other kids. It isn't fair to the other kids."

Jeff S., Daddy of One

"A kid will do what a kid can do. To run your fatherhood believing anything else is just plain stupid"

Jeff S., Daddy of One

For the grandparents, *I would like to advise that each visit should help the parents, rather than being a burden. When you visit your son or daughter with their newborn, call or plan ahead. Offer to stop at the store and pick up whatever they need. Or just bring a casserole, salad, or healthy dessert (disposable container or U-Clean.) A package of disposable diapers or an offer to pay for the diaper delivery is sure to be welcome, but check which the parents prefer.*

This is a wonderful time to share stories of your son or daughter's babyhood or childhood. You will probably never have a more receptive audience. Let them know how important they are to you, even while you talk about the less agreeable parts -- was it hard to get them to sleep through the night? Did they have allergies? Did they have strong food preferences? How about the time their grand-mommy could not get them to stop crying when she was babysitting? These stories reinforce the idea that raising a baby is hard work, but that it usually turns out just right, and that nature programmed it to be one of life's greatest rewards.

Times have changed, and your son or daughter may do some things differently than you did. That is their right and their privilege. After you have told them what worked for you, respect their choices. Ask what you can do, and love those grandchildren! That is really what it is all about.

*Eleanor W., Mommy of Two
and Grandma of Two, WA*

Resources

The songs, craft ideas, recipes and such were brought about in many forms. My research did not include books but rather hands-on experience and generous donations. Many came from my years of personal experience as an Early Childhood Educator of young children. Some were formulated as an on-the-job Mommy. The rest were kindly donated to me by other Moms and Dads. Although many of the Moms and Dads who shared their tricks and tips chose to be anonymous a few graciously allowed me to include their names in print. It is here that I wish to give credit to these hardworking and creative parents.

Gina C., Mommy of Two, New Jersey
Carol I., Mommy of Two, New Jersey
Noelle P., Mommy of One, North Carolina
Barbara S., Mommy of Three, New Jersey
Dave I., Daddy of Three, New Jersey
Ginger C., Mommy of Two, New Jersey
Patricia I., Mommy of Three, New Jersey
LaDonna E., Mommy of Two, Kentucky
Rachel, Mommy of Three, United Kingdom
Layla R., Mommy of One, Georgia
Eleanor W., Mommy of Two/Grandma of Two, WA
Jeff S., Daddy of One
Trina T., Mommy of Two, New Jersey

Printed in the United States
5740